PLOUGH W9-AYS-157

Spring 2005 · Vol. 31, No. 1

GUEST EDITOR
Martín Espada

EDITOR
Don Lee

MANAGING EDITOR
Robert Arnold

POETRY EDITOR
David Daniel

ASSOCIATE FICTION EDITOR
Maryanne O'Hara

FOUNDING EDITOR
DeWitt Henry

FOUNDING PUBLISHER
Peter O'Malley

ADVISORY EDITORS

Sherman Alexie
Russell Banks
Charles Baxter
Ann Beattie
Madison Smartt Bell
Anne Bernays
Frank Bidart
Amy Bloom
Robert Boswell
Henry Bromell
Rosellen Brown
James Carroll
Madeline DeFrees
Mark Doty
Rita Dove
Stuart Dybek
Cornelius Eady
Carolyn Forché
Richard Ford
George Garrett
Lorrie Goldensohn
Mary Gordon
Jorie Graham
David Gullette
Marilyn Hacker

Donald Hall
Joy Harjo
Stratis Haviaras
DeWitt Henry
Jane Hirshfield
Alice Hoffman
Fanny Howe
Marie Howe
Gish Jen
Justin Kaplan
Bill Knott
Yusef Komunyakaa
Maxine Kumin
Philip Levine
Margot Livesey
Thomas Lux
Gail Mazur
Campbell McGrath
Heather McHugh
James Alan McPherson
Sue Miller
Lorrie Moore
Paul Muldoon
Jay Neugeboren
Howard Norman

Tim O'Brien
Joyce Peseroff
Carl Phillips
Jayne Anne Phillips
Robert Pinsky
Alberto Ríos
Lloyd Schwartz
Jane Shore
Charles Simic
Gary Soto
Elizabeth Spires
Maura Stanton
Gerald Stern
Mark Strand
Christopher Tilghman
Richard Tillinghast
Chase Twichell
Fred Viebahn
Ellen Bryant Voigt
Dan Wakefield
Derek Walcott
Alan Williamson
Tobias Wolff
C. D. Wright
Al Young

PLOUGHSHARES, a journal of new writing, is guest-edited serially by prominent writers who explore different and personal visions, aesthetics, and literary circles. PLOUGHSHARES is published in April, August, and December at Emerson College, 120 Boylston Street, Boston, MA 02116-4624. Telephone: (617) 824-8753. Web address: www.pshares.org.

ASSISTANT FICTION EDITOR: Jay Baron Nicorvo. EDITORIAL ASSISTANTS: Elizabeth Parfitt and Laura Wareck. BOOKSHELF ADVISORS: Cate Marvin and Fred Leebron. PROOFREADER: Megan Weireter.

POETRY READERS: Simeon Berry, Autumn McClintock, Kathleen Rooney, Zachary Sifuentes, Chris Tonelli, Elisa Gabbert, Erin Lavelle, Tracy Gavel, Jen Thurber, and Megan Weireter. FICTION READERS: Gregg Rosenblum, Nicole Kelly, Hannah Bottomy, Sara Wittleton, Jessica Keener, Leslie Busler, Matthew Modica, Ashley Joseph O'Shaughnessy, Kathleen Rooney, Asako Serizawa, Simeon Berry, Eson Kim, Wendy Wunder, Emily Ekle, Erin Lavelle, Dan Medeiros, Marin Buschel, Leslie Cauldwell, James Charlesworth, Cortney Hamilton, Susan Nusser, Emily Santolla, Patricia Reed, Brenda Pike, Laura McCune-Poplin, and Steve Himmer.

SUBSCRIPTIONS (ISSN 0048-4474): $24 for one year (3 issues), $46 for two years (6 issues); $27 a year for institutions. Add $12 a year for international ($10 for Canada).

UPCOMING: Fall 2005, a fiction issue edited by Antonya Nelson, will appear in August 2005. Winter 2005–06, a poetry and fiction issue edited by David St. John, will appear in December 2005.

SUBMISSIONS: Reading period is from August 1 to March 31 (postmark dates). All submissions sent from April to July are returned unread. Please see page 218 for editorial and submission policies.

Back-issue, classroom-adoption, and bulk orders may be placed directly through PLOUGHSHARES. Microfilms of back issues may be obtained from University Microfilms. PLOUGHSHARES is also available as CD-ROM and full-text products from EBSCO, H.W. Wilson, Information Access, and UMI. Indexed in M.L.A. Bibliography, American Humanities Index, Index of American Periodical Verse, Book Review Index. Full publisher's index is online at www.pshares.org. The views and opinions expressed in this journal are solely those of the authors. All rights for individual works revert to the authors upon publication.

PLOUGHSHARES receives support from the National Endowment for the Arts and the Massachusetts Cultural Council.

Retail distribution by Ingram Periodicals and Bernhard DeBoer. Printed in the U.S.A. on recycled paper by Capital City Press.

© 2005 by Emerson College   ISBN 1-933058-00-5

CONTENTS

Spring 2005

CONTENTS

Cover art:
Detail from *The Calling II* by
Maria Magdalena Campos-Pons
Large format Polaroids, two panels,
20″ x 24″ each, 2003

Ploughshares Patrons

This nonprofit publication would not be possible without the
support of our readers and the generosity of the following
individuals and organizations.

COUNCIL
William H. Berman
Denise and Mel Cohen
Robert E. Courtemanche
Jeff and Jan Greenhawt
Jacqueline Liebergott
Turow Foundation
Eugenia Gladstone Vogel
Marillyn Zacharis

PATRON
Linda C. Wisnewski
William Collatos Family Foundation

FRIENDS
Robert Hildreth
Tom Jenks and Carol Edgarian
Howard M. Liberman
Patrick O'Brien
Christopher and Colleen Palermo

ORGANIZATIONS
Emerson College
Lannan Foundation
Massachusetts Cultural Council
National Endowment for the Arts

Introduction

I began editing this issue of *Ploughshares* in the summer of 2004, shortly after my return from Chile, where I was invited, with Yusef Komunyakaa and Nathalie Handal, to participate in the celebration of the Neruda Centenary.

We had entered the Republic of Poetry. Restaurants used Neruda's odes for recipes, and proudly announced this fact on the menu. Radio call-in shows debated the merits of political poetry versus love poetry. There were séances to communicate with poet-spirits. A group of young poets, called Casagrande, who once rented a helicopter and bombarded the national palace in Santiago with poems on bookmarks, was plotting to commit the same act in Guernica. A security guard at the Santiago airport discovered that I was a poet and wouldn't let me through the line until I recited a poem for her.

Most tellingly, the families of the disappeared—those imprisoned and murdered by the Pinochet regime—staged a demonstration at Neruda's tomb in the midst of the celebration, demanding to know the fate of their loved ones and calling for the killers to be punished. Of course they should bring their appeal for justice to the grave of a poet. For these citizens of the Republic of Poetry, it made perfect sense.

In October, I visited Walt Whitman's house in Camden, New Jersey. Whitman was Neruda's poetic father, and mine, too. Pablo would have been shocked. Compared to Neruda's house at Isla Negra—an astonishing museum and a national treasure—Whitman's house is spare and solitary, overlooking a prison across the street. On this day, five people trailed behind a tour guide who seemed more preoccupied with Whitman's chairs than the poet himself. The priorities of the two governments, and the two cultures, were starkly illustrated.

Yet we are also a republic of poets, and a nation of storytellers. In this age of the illiterate presidency, there is an increasingly urgent need for expression through the written word. There are more good poems and stories being produced, and consumed—nay, devoured—in this country than ever before. If this is a funeral, then it's a jazz funeral.

This issue of *Ploughshares* is proof. The writers in these pages not only demonstrate the health of their craft; they also create a record of their times. Their language is powerful precisely because it is not the language of power. Phrases such as "weapons of mass destruction," and their devious uses by our government to rationalize war, bleed language of its meaning. The poems and stories herein restore the blood to words.

Thus, the writers speak against the war in Iraq, but ultimately against war and occupation everywhere: in Palestine, Viet Nam, Korea, and the world. The writers protest against the violations of human decency in the cells of Abu Ghraib, but also recall the disappeared of Chile and a lynching victim in Mississippi. The writers confront authority in the form of the military and the police, but also in the form of violence in the family. The writers deal with poverty from the streets of contemporary Paris to the New Hampshire countryside in the Depression. Whitman's prisoners and slaves populate these pages; the writers accept the responsibility of making the invisible visible.

There are other eternal struggles here: against time, illness, aging, death. There are countless absurdities that catch the eye: a brawl over a chess match, the journeys of a giant cheese, the haggling over an apartment ruined in the wake of 9/11, vomit on the shoes of a minor television celebrity.

At the same time, these writers find so much to praise. There are two odes from Neruda himself, marking the occasion of his centenary, to the eye and to the elephant, respectively. There are praise-poems for the guitar, a mortar and pestle, a mockingbird, a young couple in the grass, a singing father, a beloved poet, strange and beautiful words. The writers love the same world that causes them so much grief.

This is the world I collected in a big cardboard box that I dragged from room to room for months. I read manuscripts through October and watched the Red Sox stage their stirring comeback against the Yankees to take the American League pennant, then stampede the Cardinals to win their first World Series since 1918. Here, after eighty-six years, after the miraculous defeat of an aristocratic and arrogant tormentor, was something like justice. If the Red Sox could vanquish the Yankees and go on to win the World Series, could other dreams deferred be far off?

At a breakfast joint in Boston where I waited for the Red Sox victory parade to begin, I encountered a waitress from Ireland dressed in a Manny Ramirez jersey. At the table everyone talked about the Red Sox as metaphor, representing the infinite possibilities of change for the good. "Like peace in Ireland," someone said. The waitress shot back: "There will never be peace in Ireland." So much for infinite possibilities.

Indeed, President Bush was reelected soon afterwards. Unlike those who swore they would flee to Canada after this national embarrassment, I calmly decided that I was never leaving my house again. I was left with my cardboard box. I dipped into the box and fished out more metaphors, with gratitude.

Someday, when peace and justice come to Ireland, their poets and storytellers will be there. Neruda wrote during the Spanish Civil War: "The world has changed and my poetry has changed." Indeed, the world has changed many of the writers collected in this issue of *Ploughshares;* yet, many of these same writers will change the world by changing the people who read them, in ways great and small, profound and subtle.

JACK AGÜEROS

Mouth Full of Words

I woke up this morning with my mouth full of words
Like "Crenellated battlements," and cranciousness
And bicycles with "derailleur" and flywheels and tappets.

These words must be escapees from where they grew bored.
Stuck in the same old sentences they decided to break out
And now they are fugitives in my mouth and ears.

Unruly, untidy, possibly misspelled
I want to unspell them and respell them
And wrangle and trample them,

Make them all mean nothing or everything
Who cares what meaning I attach to them
When they ride into my ears and camp?

I don't say anything but "welcome words"
Whatever you mean, wherever you go
I want to be there trying to decipher you.

O words, mitoctousstly dividing
In my mouth, perhaps I do not know
Your meaning, but I love your taste, your sound.

NIN ANDREWS

What the Therapist Said

Just because you think a man is dead
doesn't mean you should leave him.
Really, the dead have a lot of advantages
over the living. Think about your dad.
How much better you get along with him
now that he's passed. It's time's way.
And why in the end everything turns out okay.
A lot of women would envy you. The dead,
let's be honest, they're pretty stiff fellows.
And you don't have to worry about talking to them.
You can if you want to of course. You said
the one thing you *do* talk about
is how you both hate George Bush.
I imagine all the dead hate Bush. Too bad
they don't vote anymore. But that's something.
It's a start. Besides, in these parts
most of the living men are Republicans.
Really, I'd think twice about this.
Whether you'd like to spend your life
with a man who's dead or alive. It's a tough choice.

Hole

One morning they dig up the sidewalk and leave
No sign of the truck
only the large
dark shadow digging and digging
piling up sludge with a hand shovel
beside the only tree
Two o'clock I come by
and he's slumbering in the grass beside rat holes
Three and he's stretched across a jagged stone wall
folded hands tucked beneath one ear
a beautiful young boy smiling
not the heavy large shadow who can't breathe
Four-thirty and the August heat
takes one down here
He's pulled up an elbow joint
some three feet round
At seven I head home for the night
pass the fresh gravel mound
a soft footprint near the manhole
like the "x" *abuelo* would place beside his name
all the years he couldn't write

Time as a Verb

This is the way
I describe it; what time does
to hands and face.
              That old-timer
shoots a glance that makes
like God in Genesis, you—
a very image and withered
likeness.
              Or a finger points, mocking
the way hands dislocate
dates, memories, who's died, what voices
issue from one-way traffic—souls
like a hum on a highway.

"Cheat"
is maybe a sound verb.

And don't talk gradualism;
that pro holds a winning hand;
(Genesis, verse one).

He flicks cards face up—
it's a lightning bolt, shark smile,
winner take all.

And you're like Merton
struck dumb on the instant—
the sheer skill of it, the nerve—

and you wear
a loser's look forever.

Or like me
not quite everything lost,
shirt now, shroud later.

Another instance—
time as verb.

What's Love Got to Do?

All summer *Papá* holds a cigarette out the window of his laser-green Buick, points his lips left to blow the smoke into the mirage of exhaust between rush-hour cars. All summer he listens to *La Cubanisima* on AM radio exploding with accounts of how Castro took everything *we* had, how *we'd* get it back someday. All summer he wears polyester ties and his over-polished loafers. All summer I float my arm like a wing out the window as we glide down Coral Way, past storefronts and memories: the 7-11 stops for Blow-Pops and Slurpees, the square pizzas at Frankie's, the birthday dinners at Canton Rose. All summer I want to ask if he remembers what I remember, but I don't, so he just drives, all summer, keeping a safe distance in the right lane, from our Miami suburb to my uncle's *bodega,* where all summer I price and rotate, mop and bag and save for my own car. All summer I don't want to be me. I don't want to be my father either, eleven years in his windowless office adding and subtracting, wishing and forgetting he could be more. All summer he picks me up at 6:00 and we drive back on the same road, the same mix of cigarettes and piña colada air-freshener, the same visors eclipsing our faces, the same silence. All summer I wait for him to say something—anything, like: *I hate grapefruit juice,* or *I can't stand the Navarros,* or *I've cheated on your mother,* or *I hate this life.* What he did say was: *I love Tina Turner,* every time I took control of the radio and tuned in to her FM hits. All summer he sang along in his thick Cuban accent (*waus love gotta do / gotta do wis it*) and whistle through the words he didn't know. Then he'd say something about *Mamá* and him in the sixties dancing to Ike and Tina in Cuba, and pick up the refrain again (*waus love but a secon' hand emoshun*). He embarrassed me with his singing all summer, that summer before his throat swelled, before the weekly visits to Dr. Morad, before the mitomycin and Hail Marys failed, before he'd never sing again. That summer, when all I managed to mutter was: *Yeah, I love Tina, too.*

MICHELLE BOISSEAU

A Sunday in God Years

Like someone trying to nap in a room
with a glaring terrarium
God rolls over
but before resuming his dream
where He's a lover
decked out in a sunbeam,
He glances at the blue planet
he made, at continents crashing
and mountains popping up, at sheets of dirt
settling in streams and streams
settling in oceans that slide back
like bedcovers and after stacks
of pressing epochs give birth

in an outcrop to this ragged chunk
of limestone. I plucked it
from a wall fading into the woods
of Northern Kentucky.
Ordovician, half a billion years old.
It was the common rock of my childhood,
what we pried from yards and pulled
from creeks to flush out crawdads
scuttling beneath. That's an hour's drive
and forty years ago, on the north side
of the Ohio. River Jordan. Promised Land.
Fine heft, a good fit to my hand,
the rock's finger notches are the curves
of river bends on a map—it's shaped
like Kentucky—and here's the turn
the river takes, *wade*
in the water, on its way

north from Maysville, here a cove
where a runaway could hide—
her child slung in a shawl—studying the floes
until the moon set and she could plunge
across the bobbing ice
to board, *sweet chariot,* the train of trudging—
cornfields, torches, disquieting towns, huddling
in root cellars by day, then in the hull
of a midnight boat slipping across Lake
Erie. The rock I slid from the wall
was stacked here by a slave. And slaves
felled trees, broke sod, and cut the stone
for foundations they couldn't own.

Up on the ancient hill the grand old house
they built is solitary now.
The clutter of shacks for those who worked
sun and snow, day and night
have long been erased as eyesores
although the played-out double-wides
along the road tell a revised story.
And as for me, a middle-aged white
woman, I didn't have to care
who'd notice me helping myself
to these grainy eons, plunder
embedded with the trails and shells
of creatures seen by no eye although carelessly
glanced long ago through warm shallow
seas by a younger sun.

KEVIN BOWEN

The Second Night

Outside the white cottage, a half-dozen chairs set out.
A run of rocky fields washed by starlight.

Full moon rising off the cliffs
cutting a path to the islands.

Inside the cottage, the sounds of children
quieting themselves.

The slow scrape and rattle of chairs
dragged across a linoleum floor.

Last stir of footsteps fading softly
down a darkened road.

A face pressed against glass
stealing a last look out a window.

One night ending.
A second night begins.

Arriving

We're newcomers to an old place. The house
was built in 1860 (so we think);
since then, the Portuguese fishermen
and the faded, artsy bohemians
have come and started now to go, replaced
by "guppies" driving Lexuses. Our street
is lined with lindens, home to chickadees
that play in the elaborate display
of whirligigs, birdbaths, wind chimes, and what's
got to be the world's most complex bird feeder
constructed by the man who lived next door
year-round, until at eighty-eight he died
of what the rumors say was "just pneumonia."
Being doctors, we are privy to much more
than other weekenders with second homes:
we know about the prostate three doors down;
across the street, it's diabetic feet
and cataracts. Some friends who've seen our place
have asked us when another like it might
become available; we sipped our drinks
beneath the twilit sky, approving of
the light, the certain quality it has
that no one could articulate. Ice clinked
as if in harmony with the cascade
of notes from those wind chimes next door; I knew
the realtors had been there yesterday.
Another neighbor down the street has AIDS,
as if to prove us not so different—
"They told me I could live with it," he'd said,
"for twenty years—and now I get lymphoma,"
while well-fed birds bounced from above like balls
belonging to the gods' unruly children.
Arriving here, perhaps like us he thought

he might escape; perhaps he sought the light
the artists and the Portuguese came here
to venerate in each their human way.
Expatriates like them, I want to say...
A painting we admired on a cold day,
off-season, on Commercial Street: two men
working nets in a small boat, churning sea,
the light between them captured perfectly,
belonging, it might seem, to everyone.
We left the gallery and headed home.

Making Sense of the Currency
on Line for Le Musée Picasso

However closer it might seem to art—
the brightly colored bills, the graceful figures
about to waltz off heavy coins—it pays for
the gasoline, the decaf and baguette.
To use a public toilet costs two francs,
a little less than what I give the man
without a leg whose sign I understand
(another universal language, inked
in French, called poverty and suffering)—
the smell of money, like the smell of piss,
is recognizable in any place.
For thirty francs, we're in: like broken things
too priceless to be thrown away, we see
Picassos everywhere, stark misery.

Clarinet

At the stained window,
a morning jay.
I stop my scissoring,
as if I could reclaim
a Santiago of bird-call
and sudden ease,
as if I could annul
the battle-gray maze of gutting
jails, courthouses, morgues—
purgatory where I bend
over the burlap,
again and again,
to show the world
the smashed black bell
of your clarinet.

A blue swatch
of your workshirt becomes
the raw dusk of that day;
here, in this farrago of scraps,
your room as I found it:
Lunatic with ripped songsheets...

In imploring red,
a beggar's vermilion,
I have stitched:
Whoever sees this arpillera,
help me to pray for my son.
He was seen leaving rehearsal
at 7 o'clock.
He was seen in detention
at Londres #38.
He was seen, he was seen...

After eleven years,
Carlos,
perhaps you wouldn't recognize me;
I've become the weatherworn,
undocile woman
manacled to a tyrant's fence,
a mother dancing the *gueca* solo
in the monitored plaza,
the ache of my make-do arms
trumpeted,
your rakish college photo
pinned to my blouse:
in the *arpillera,*
a tiny appliquéd doll
forever mourning,
Carlos,
forever swaying
to an unforgettable woodwind.

More than Peace and Cypresses

More than peace and cypresses, emboldened
hares at the field's edge,

Father, I love
gallantry, tenacity, the sanguine

heart before the ledge:
the artist questing and failing—

the feet of bested Icarus
plunging into the sea's crest—

the artist triumphing: a page of fire
from the book of heroes.

More than light-hooved gazelles, views
from the mizzenmast,

enlivening shores,
more than soldier-still lilies, I love

the torchlike men who've taught me—
past the rueful

glitter of lucre and guns,
past the starkness of the lynching tree—

the truth-or-bust beauty
of passion transformed

into sheer compassion,
true shouldering,

and common as breath, common as breath,
the extravagant wheel of birth and death.

NAN COHEN

Abraham and Isaac: I

He took him outside and said, "Look toward heaven
and count the stars, if you are able to count them."
And He added, "So shall your offspring be."

I have lived in tents and know how faint a trace
we leave behind us on the earth;
how, when the body fails, the soul folds
its light clothes and steals away.

But now a child sleeps in my tent;
I would raise a tower of stone to shield his head,
and yet the thought that any common stone
must outlast him provokes such rage in me

I wake all night, alarmed and furious,
seeing nothing in the dark but dark.

Abraham and Isaac: II

And Abraham picked up the knife to slay his son

I have lived in tents and often, at midday,
have I parted the tent-clothes and gone inside
with the light of day so blinding my eyes
that my wife spoke to me out of darkness,
saying, Take this dish, and eat.

I have walked among the flocks on starless nights
with the blackness so filling my eyes
I put forth my hand,
as if the night were a tent,
as if some shape might glimmer in my sight
before the cloths of night fell across it.

Eyes full of light or dark,
night or day, I cannot tell.
I grope forward to lift the cloth
of this moment, and the next.

Pentecost in Little Falls, New Jersey

If I arrived early, I had to listen
To hundreds of sewing machines
Spiraling their high-pitched arias
Up against the mill's metal shell.

Each woman, a soloist withdrawn
Into her small cubicle of work,
Sang the crazy hope of piecework—
Another zipper, another dollar.

A wall chart traced their numbers
In money's green line. It didn't
Record the pain when someone
Ran the needle through her finger.

I came at noon—between classes
At the state college where I read
Marx, and daydreamed revolution—
To eat lunch with my grandmother.

Exactly at noon, there was a moment
Of quiet between the machines
Shutting down and the women rising
In common with their bag lunches.

They gathered at long metal tables.
High above them, a narrow strip
Of eave windows gave the only sign
Of weather and, sun or gloom,

Let down a long flume of light
In which the women's bodies

Slowly relaxed, their lunches spread
Before them, and the patter of talk

Began in all those different tongues—
Haitian Creole, Canadian French,
Mexican and Puerto Rican Spanish,
Polish, Romanian, English,

Jamaican English—that spoke as one
The gospel of sacrifice and hard work.
They shared frayed photographs,
Smoked, spread the good news

Of children and grandchildren,
This one smart as a whip, this one
Taking dance lessons, this one a sight
To see hitting a baseball. There were

Some they worried about collectively,
And one who actually gave up booze
And became the man of their prayers.
Many more, of course, would not

Be saved no matter how hard
They worked. No end to the curses
And slammed doors, the hands
And faces bloodied by impotence

And rage. I often left the mill
Wondering if their hard ritual
Of work-eat-sleep-work ever changed
The state of daily lousiness at all.

The women believed, or had to
Believe. Over thirty years ago,
And still I see them returning to
Their machines, the unforgiving

Clock running once again,
The women bending to their work,
Losing themselves freely in that noisy
Oblivion because each of them

Cradles a secret happiness—that someone,
Working at his own sweet time,
Might tell the story many years later
Of how he had come to be saved.

ROBERT CREELEY

Old Story

from *The Diary of Francis Kilvert*

One bell wouldn't ring loud enough.
So they beat the bell to hell, Max,
with an axe, show it who's boss,
boss. Me, I dreamt I dwelt in
someplace one could relax
but I was wrong, wrong, *wrong*.
You got a song, man, sing it.
You got a bell, man, ring it.

The Red Flower

What one thinks to hold
Is what one thinks to know,
So comes of simple hope
And leads one on.

The others there the same
With no one then to blame
These flowered circles handed.
So each in turn was bonded.

There the yellow bees will buzz,
And eyes and ears appear
As listening, witnessing hearts
Of each who enters here.

Yet eyes were closed—
As if the inside world one chose
To live in only as one knows.
No thing comes otherwise.

Walk on, on crippled leg,
Because one stumped with cane,
Turned in and upside down
As with all else, bore useless weight.

The way from here is there
And back again, from birth to death,
From egg to echo, flesh to eyeless skull.
One only sleeps to breathe.

The hook, the heart, the body
Deep within its dress, the folds of feelings,
Face to face to face, no bandaged simple place,
No wonder more than this, none less.

Misremembering the Classics

There's spit on my face and a smirking
    sixteen-year-old
        with a cross tattooed on each eyelid
waiting to see what comes next.

    Reggie's got three inches,
        fifty pounds on me,
but as I wait for backup
    that doesn't come, I know

    that, like me,
he's a sorry mix
    of testosterone and fear.
        Alarms and red lights play

on broken glass from the chair-splintered
    nursing station window,
        there's no staff to bail us out,
everyone's pinning kids down

    like some high-school wrestling match
        gone crazy, and for some reason,
as we wait for things to play out,
    I ask about the book on his bed,

    The Call of the Wild.
Once, I say, when I was sixteen
    I found myself in a blizzard,
        and because I recalled

Jack London's "To Build a Fire"
    and how the hero burrowed
        into a drift to keep from freezing,
I dug a bed in the warm snow.

    Reggie's stopped listening, he's crumbling
        a ceiling tile in his hands,
shouts "Get out! Now!"
    and I do,

    I wait outside his room,
our uneasy compromise
    until the police arrive
        and the hospital's finally calmed.

Next day, in his battered room
    I finish my story,
        tell how I reread London
years later and realized the guy

    who slept in that snowstorm
        died. Grudging laughter,
so I ask Reggie-the-book-reader
    if he ever writes, and yes, he's a poet.

    My challenge, then,
while he serves his day of seclusion:
    If your life is 100% crap,
        let every word be only pain.

But say your life is fifty-fifty,
    be honest, make half the images positive,
        get your girlfriend in there,
write something that makes you laugh.

By shift's end he's managed
      forty bleak lines, but the last one's
about a sparrow in the hospital garden
    screwing around and singing after the rain stops.

    I ask him to read
the poem a second time. Crude, rough,
    fine. It's what we've got
      to work with.

RICHARD GARCIA

My Grandmother's Laughter

My grandmother's laughter was an exploding plate,
the kind that the traveling salesman said
would never break, and he'd fling it against the kitchen floor
just to prove his point, and the plate would spin
making a kind of high-pitched whine.
My grandmother's laughter was like that, too; almost soundless,
like it was running out of breath, a stillness
astonished at itself, the quiet eye of a hurricane.
My grandmother's hands fluttered like pigeons
on a window ledge when I was falling asleep.
Her eyes were the color of accordion music.
She listened to Sergeant Preston of the Yukon,
read, over and over, *Anne of Green Gables*
and *Tarzan, King of the Jungle.*
I never saw her picture staring at me from the mantel.
Are you my grandmother? I would ask her.
Sure, kid, she'd mumble, a cigar clenched between her teeth,
and then she'd hoist her shotgun up and blast
another of those unbreakable Melmac plates
that I would throw up in the air into smithereens.
Fuchi, that stinks, she would say
when she stuck her head in the kitchen
where my mother was cooking menudo, *huele feo.*
Because she always told the truth her shins never hurt.
She told me she could ask a question of her special spirit
and an image of the answer would appear in a bubble of light.
She said that President Truman was an estupid son-of-a-bitchie.
My grandmother only read newspapers of the future.
Sometimes she made me so happy, I had nightmares to
     compensate.
She would walk into my dreams and sell me magazine
     subscriptions—
me, known as El Diablo, the one who spits in the mirror,

who cried in the womb, who fathered his own grandmother,
he of the silent fire escapes and forensic closet dust.
Looking up from the Ouija board, she leaned over
and whispered in my ear, You will have no descendants
and be a disgrace to your many grandchildren.
Ani routsay ooga, I answered, not knowing
that I had just asked for cake in the language of Jesus.
Only I could break the unbreakable plates without a shotgun.
That is why the plates spoke to me. You will never
have a grandmother, they said. It's true,
my grandmother added, blasting another plate
out of the sky. It was blue, and pieces of it rained down on me
like pieces of an angel, some beautiful, goddamned angel,
    shot out of the sky.

The Battle of Lepanto

artist unknown, Venice

It's an enormous canvas. Beyond rows of oars
men stab
and thrust, grab
each other's throats, pitch bodies into the water

where they sink or else are driven under
by keels
and pikes. It feels
odd standing in this great hall where

another tourist is being warned, *No photograph.*
The flash
gives away the trust
violated—one guard just isn't enough

in a room this size. People do whatever
they can get away
with. Say
what you want, but there it is. In a room I left, from a corner

behind this huge, dark imposing door
I heard voices
arguing. This nice
young guy continued calmly narrating into his camcorder

while his girlfriend (I'm guessing) fussed into his ear.
Maybe she was angry
already, or maybe
she heard me coming and didn't want repeated what I saw

occur to them in a different room: a guard come over
and place his palm
over the viewfinder. No harm
was done, but you could see the guard meant business where

obeying the rules was concerned. Off the coast of Greece, Don Juan
of Austria led the Christian League
of Venetian and Spanish galleys
against the Turks under Ali Pasha, their commander-in-chief, in a war

that would determine commercial and political power
for centuries to come.
Never mind who won.
There were 8,000 Christian and 25,000 Turkish martyrs.

Scent: Love Poem for the Pilón

I thank God for el Mercado, in Santurce,
where we filled our bags.
I thank God for the chopped translucence of onions
above which we poured oregano & salt.
& I thank God for yellow oil in the pot,
the buckle & hiss of heat under a pan.

I am thankful for the kitchen table:
block of wood, & nails,
& the carpenter's hand.
I thank God for cloves.
       I am thankful for red beans & black beans.
& rice. I am thankful for rice.
& I am thankful for the barking of dogs
like the ones we'd sometimes hear
outside the window above the sink.

I am thankful for fruits in bowls,
the wet of faucet, the way clean dishes went
on the left side, dirty dishes on the right.

I thank God for the chopping board, & light,
the grind of pepper going *chekere! chekere!*
& the clean smell of tomatoes & cilantro.
& I thank God for the pilón
that burst the knots of garlic,
thankful for the way it always worked & worked
under a fist. How, even now, after washes with limes
& soaps, the scent of what it's opened
still lingers there.

The Law

Avila, 1982

When the civil guards approached me
and asked me for my papers,

I recalled the face of a sunny saint
being disemboweled on the rack.

Widows in perennial black, addicts of prayer,
find comfort here the way monks

in hair shirts must take to penance,
or me, addled in my blissed-out days

in San Francisco, tugging daily on a roach.
And that's how I must've been,

befogged in Avila on a visit
that coincided with the papal tour.

A murder of crows, clerics, nuns in wimples,
tarring the field with their black habits.

St. Frances de Sales dispenses, "The measure
of love is to love without measure."

This republic of goodness
was once peopled with spies. Maybe

that's what got the saints in trouble,
their willingness to surrender

once found out. I know authority
when I see it make a U-turn to pull me over.

I also know that the Burgos Christ
in its pageant red skirt is tethered to a story,

its weals and welts, blueblack,
the wounds Nicodemus witnessed as he

lowered Jesus, alone in his discarded body.
The carving by Nicodemus

would one day float its way
first to a monastery, then to Burgos.

When the civil guards approached me
and asked me for my papers,

I felt for a string around my neck, my scapular
like a leaf pressed on the road of pistils and stamens.

That moment stood
for something I can no longer recall.

What with those men and their gift
of whiteness, their constant need of proof.

I must've smiled at them, clueless yet longing
to be profound.

DONALD HALL

Bread and Butter

In 1936, when a tramp knocked on the farmhouse door
and asked, please, for bread and butter, Kate

hacked him a slice from the loaf she baked
last Wednesday, and spread on it the Holstein butter

she churned Saturday morning. He thanked her, Ma'am,
and walked down the road looking for Help Wanted,

for a sawmill starting up, for an outhouse to clean,
for a nation of buttered bread, a roof, and a fat wife.

SAM HAMILL

Arguing with Milosz in Vilnius

You are recently dead, old man,
    with your thunderous brows
and voice like a vast sea
    hinting at a dangerous undertow—
you are gone, your generation
    of testimony, of witness,
gone, gone among the ancient rites
    of passage, gone,
taking with you the innumerable
    names of the lost.

And yet I am here, walking
    the broad, freshly bricked avenue
of a democratic Vilnius,
    the Mother Sun
pouring amber on a world
    you would barely recognize,
where women are the ones
    dressed to kill, and the world
does what it will to be reborn.
    The poet is reborn
on each new old street,
    born in the process of the song.
You gave me Anna Swir.

Do you remember how we argued
    in Berkeley
when you told me, "I dislike nature,"
    and said it again
in comments on your beloved Jeffers—
    "a huge museum of inherited images"—
and how could I not remember that
    as I rode in a van to Druskininkai?

How I loved the slender birches
    among the red pine,
the forest floor a bed of moss
    and a hundred kinds of mushrooms.
Bury a trout in mushrooms,
    cream and wine,
and bake it, and hear me sigh.

And you were with me again
    in "Scoundrel Square"
(I renamed it) where the sculptures
    of the Soviet regime
provide inherited imagery
    of another kind, museum
of our agonies and tragedies where
    I knew once again
that your world
    could not be mine—
and yet I am here, the bland faces
    and stern faces—Russian, Lithuanian—
of ordinary men who sold
    their countrymen for a song
are carved into my mind.

Tyranny is so banal.
    Jackdaws clack and squabble.
Sparrows flock to the square.
    Lenin Boulevard is gone.
I cross the square at the cathedral
    and turn up a narrow cobbled street,
Old Town, tiled roofs
    and freshly painted shutters,
where a hundred vendors will,
    in an hour or so,
present their wares to tourists.
    Four hundred thousand people
disappeared. Each had a name,
    a life filled with passion
and despair and all those

   ordinary irritations
too small and too many
      to enumerate—
It's more than one mind's heart can bear.

And yet the same brown river flows
      quietly between the same banks
as it did a thousand years ago.
      Here, it turns north.
Where is Bakszta Street? Where
      is Antokol? I sat
in the courtyard of the old monastery
      you so long ago admired,
the bench a little askew, grass overgrown,
      but a sanctuary from
the relentless noise of the city,
      as my friend Mindaugas explained
how you sought refuge here
      long before the war.
Was there a certain guilt
      from having merely survived?
Is it criminal to be lucky?

You were right, of course.
      "The struggle for poetry in the world
cannot take place in a museum."
      And the fact that you reject,
out of hand, my "eastern wisdom"
      also does not offend.
As little as I knew you, I knew
      you well enough to learn.
Our friend Rexroth introduced us
      on the streets of that great city
you came to call "nearly a home."
      You were a totem, an icon, a teacher.
Nevertheless, I say the world's a museum,
      the poem a record of survival
and betrayal, of human longing—
      vision and commitment—

and if I smell the bear or the wolf
    that once haunted the woods near here,
I say the wolf is alive
    in the eyes of men, alive
in the hearts of all who survive.

You were a great exile of the war;
    I was merely an orphan.
You were a child of Vilnius,
    of Europe; I was a child
of the wilderness of the west
    and know the track of the wolf,
the terrible odor of bear. Nevertheless,
    you civilized me some.
You were a great modernist,
    full of conviction,
sometimes a little short on patience.
    I could not fully grasp your history
or your god. And yet I am here.
    Vive la difference!
I bow to your presence
    as I stand among the ancients.

The Warrior

It was Wednesday, I remember. Maybe it was Thursday. I had arrived early, early enough to drink some good wine alone with a man I thought we all should fear and for a second forgot. Then they arrived. Nothing in me had changed, even after the wine, even after I saw a goat and corpse cut open side by side. Some say this place is cursed, every drop of water sinks the earth. Strange the things one thinks about at moments like this—was I a stranger to the lover who saw my curves and scars, kissed them then slept like a deserter? Strange what comes to you in the dream-shadows of God—children you saw once in Nablus or Ramallah, who told you the hour the dates will grow in Palestine. Then they arrived. Announced—she died yesterday, but I heard she died a year ago, later that evening I found out she will die tomorrow. And then I heard him say, *Shut up, there is only one way to fight a war. Become the other.* I cross my legs and take his face apart trying to find a way to remember this moment otherwise.

Undertones

The sail had been drawn into an
albino python hung vertically for
the town to witness. The sea too
shallow to dock. The boat   its
chipped purple belly remained
somewhat distant   solitary with
only its static reflection. The fishermen
swam to shore. Dark-brown sand   their
patterned trails to the plaza for rest. One
wore a straw hat with a wide rim floppy

as fins   the sun burned above yet
the tawny shield kept his face shadowed.
From the three buckets they showed
friends their catch   stingrays with pale
undersides like hands. Placed on rocks
gray skins spotted   pink and green
undertones from pieces of coral   seaweed
eaten when there was nothing else.

They told a story of the giant squid that almost
pulled their boat under. The ink spewed took
weeks to clean   foamy bristles against
the deck   years of tanning until it bled.
Those young men will grow old filling
their nets. Sirens will sing   love them
when overboard. Intoxication is warm
saltwater   coconut air   will-less-ness.

When all the fish were sold they toasted cold
russet bottles   drank. Women skinned   chopped.
The fish will fall into stews   onions   dendê
milk from trees over rice. Back into the sea where
the boat waited   a day turned violet. They breathed
on small waves   these fragile lives wrought with lore.

DAVID HERNANDEZ

Chess Match Ends in Fight

As one opponent calling out checkmate
an hour past midnight could crack a man

already broken and bring allegations
from his tongue, violence to his veins,

bring him to rise and hip-knock the table
so the legs screech, so the pieces quiver

and topple, the bishop a salt shaker
kissed by an elbow, bring him to blows,

to blows, to blows, to grasp the winner
and propel him through plate glass

as if a baptism in geometric water,
so the glass rains and dazzles the floor,

so he emerges from the window stunned,
lacerated, to bring blood and the lilac

breath of night, men with stars pinned
to their chests, handcuffs jiggling,

so one's booked, the other's stitched,
the coarse thread lacing up the lesions,

as and so and to bring this to this,
we will be there with our brooms.

Don't Rub Your Eyes

I understand women the way junkies understand shooting up. Feel the rush, make the pain go away, and think about the next fix. I don't know what to do when the glow wears off, when a real person floats to the surface of the dream. It's the sixties, after all, and what might be pathology in another age has become our historical mandate to fuck. I am not alone in this, although I am extreme. I am not making a case for repentance, merely saying that what I do on the bed, the grass, the table, the back seat, is what makes me forget what's under the bed, the grass. It's dark and it smells like rice paddy silt and blood. It waits to catch me between highs—chemical or sexual—and takes me down.

Donna would be beautiful if her father hadn't broken her nose. She's beautiful anyhow; long legs, dirty blond hair, beautiful breasts, and a mean streak. Someday I'll know it's not a mean streak at all, but I'm a long way from understanding feminism. Donna is two years older than me, angry at her last lover, and fond of motorcycles. She puts on her leathers and rides sixty miles south to Mexico with her bat nets tied to the rear luggage rack. She goes during the full moon, crosses the border on dirt roads without detection, deep down into Sonora where the bats that live off the cactus fruits swarm and squeak.

She spreads the bat nets over the mouth of the cave and waits. Some Yaquis out on the road see this tall woman backlit by the moon and shout *Bruja! Bruja!*, and she touches the .357 magnum she's stuffed down the front of her Levi's; but they walk on, and soon she's got specimens to bring back, this during a time before *La Migra* began to stalk the border looking for illegals and it became harder to cross. Bats are her dissertation, and she's unconsciously developing a study of bat sonar she'll sell the Navy long after we've split.

She's got mood swings that leave me speechless and she fucks like heaven. She's my older woman, although she's not much older. She's got some scars like my scars but I'm too busy trying to bury mine to see hers.

And she's hard on the heart. She's got this guy she's on and off with, a prof in the biology department who's married, so I never know when we're going to get together. I'm working hard to keep the horrors caged and she's fucking with my emotional flak jacket. She's got hold of something other than my cock and it's making me nuts. She's a jungle.

She drinks tequila and has an owl named Hoot perched on top of her refrigerator. When I come over, Hoot does this side-to-side action with his neck that means *Try to pet me and I'll take your finger off.* She's also got snakes.

We fuck and I'm happy and then we get into an argument because I say that writing is a miserable process, like an oyster making a pearl. She says, "Oysters don't feel a damn thing. Don't throw metaphors around like that." Then we fuck again and I'm okay. Then I'm not okay.

Donna has a biologist–poet–Zen-practitioner friend named Dana. I complain to Dana about Donna.

He says, "You fly with Donna, you take the grief." It is getting dark. We are getting stoned on his back porch. Drugs don't feel good anymore. Pot loosens the flak jacket and I float where I don't want to. I'm starting to have the dream, the one that will stay with me for years. I'm naked and I'm walking through the village of Nui Kim Son. It's night, and I know the Cong are close. I'm naked and I have no weapon. I shake myself awake and look out the window. I go to the fridge for beer. I chug a quart of Coors. But the shakes don't subside and memory starts to bleed through into real time.

There's a new guy in the platoon called Paulus who's got a tattoo of a little red devil on his left shoulder blade. I've gone with Paulus and Jeter to check out a small ville just east of the desert position. No one's there but an old man. The other villagers are gone—they always see us coming. The old man has refused to leave. He's plainly senile. Paulus is enraged. I don't know why—he hasn't been here long enough for that—but he grabs the old man by his shirt and shoves him down into the family bunker underneath his hooch. He yanks a grenade off his belt and pulls the pin, waits two, then rolls the grenade into the hole. The white flash, the blast of dirt and blood.

I shake myself awake and go get another beer. It's a beautiful night in Tucson but there's a red spider web stretched across the sky. No no no no no. That thing doesn't belong there.

I'm in the Student Health Center. The psychiatrist is asking me if I've had any homosexual feelings. He tells me I have to be realistic about my fantasies. I tell him I've been in a war.

He cocks his head and raises both eyebrows. "Really," he says.

I tell him I've had LSD on a number of occasions. He says, "You mean that didn't help you?" I have no idea what he means. Maybe he's tight with Timothy Leary. I say, "I feel like a reactionary," by which I mean that I don't want to take any more drugs, even at the price of seeming unhip; but he laughs like I said something funny.

Then he asks me about my mother. This is another one of those questions they have to ask. My mother is a long way away, physically and psychically.

He writes me a scrip for something called Stelazine. He picks up the phone. I try make out what he's written on his notepad. I can only make out the last line. It says, "Acute Anxiety Reaction." He puts down the phone and tells me to go to group therapy on Tuesdays at seven.

That night Donna comes by. We are naked and she hugs me from behind and takes my cock in both her hands. I don't think anything can be better. It's the orgone fix, the rush. The pain is gone and we are fucking.

She says, "You can't think worth a damn but you're a serious piece of ass." She tells me she's been doing experiments on fruit flies and it's making her insane. She tells me she wants to kill her lover's wife. "Simpering little bitch," she says. "Dresses like Joni Mitchell. Can't sing." Donna can sing.

"What are you doing with him?"

"I love him. I love his mind."

I'm getting depressed, then she reaches between my legs and cups my balls.

Next day there's a huge rally at the university main gate at Park and Third. The police have just got new riot gear and they're showing it off. Martin Carr, our de facto Maoist movement leader, is there with a bullhorn, dressed in a Mexican wedding shirt. *One Two Three Four We Don't Want Your Fucking War.* The police start to move to clear the intersection and Carr calls for us to get out of the way. They've never seen the cops with riot helmets and batons. They've never seen tear gas canisters affixed to rifles. This is 1969.

Someone breaks the window of the drugstore at Park Avenue and Third, and the cops charge the crowd. We've never seen plastic handcuffs.

I see David Roma on his face with a cop kneeling on his back. A number of people are staggering and spluttering after a good dose of tear gas. We run to the campus Christian center. Don Eckerstrom is there—these are the days before he's traded in his priest's collar for a tie-dye T-shirt—and he's directing the tear-gas victims into the kitchen, where they're spraying their faces with a dishwashing nozzle. I shout, "Don't rub your eyes." Something in the way my voice feels when I shout makes me smell rice paddies.

Outside the police have dispersed the demonstrators. There's a T-shirt lying in the street, a couple of placards with slogans. There's a pickup truck stopped on Park Ave. driven by a guy with red hair. He's screaming at the demonstrators. There's a sticker on the rear window, below the rifle racks, that reads, "University of South Viet Nam, School of Jungle Warfare." I walk over to him.

I say, "Hey, brother."

"Fucking goddamn faggots. Wish I had me a goddamn M-79."

I say, "What you don't know is you've been fucked."

"What?"

"You've been fucked, brother."

"How'd you like your teeth in a doggy bag, asshole."

"Third Battalion First Marines, I-Corps," I say.

He looks at me incredulously. "What?"

"Just like you. We were fucked, brother."

"Shit," he says, and glares at me. His mouth drops open. He pops the clutch, leaves a long burn around the corner onto Third Street. "Fuck you!" he shouts. "Fuck you, fuck you, you fuck…"

I love the way Lizzi hangs on to me on the back of the motorcycle. We've been up to Mount Lemon on the Parilla I've just bought with my GI Bill check. She's hanging on to me tight, writhing against me, trembling. I mistake this for love. I think about what we'll do when we get to her place. I park the bike and we go inside. She puts on tea. I put my arms around her and hold her breasts.

She says, "I came about five times from the vibration of the bike. Try me later."

I am depressed and out of beer when Donna shows up in her VW and shouts for me to get in. We're going down near the border.

The desert smells sweet from the rain. Tarantulas swarm across the old two-lane highway that heads south into Sonora. Donna stops the car and gets out. Low rumble of thunder over the Chiricahuas. Donna stoops and lets a tarantula crawl onto her hand, a big hairy one with a six-inch leg span. She walks over to me and tells me to open my hand.

It's spring, a year since I came home.

Run Run Run Run Run Run Run Away

When my brother tells me he's been seeing a psychiatrist, I say, "That's great, Jack."

He says, "Why—you think I'm fucked up?"

I say, "How'd you find him?"

He says, "What makes you think my psychiatrist is a man?"

Her name is Mary Pat Delmar, and Jack tells me she is brilliant. He says, "She blows me away," and I think they must be talking a lot about junior high.

"Wow."

He smiles. "I told her you'd say that."

When he tells me how beautiful she is, I say, "But not so beautiful that you have trouble concentrating?"

"She's pretty beautiful," he says. Plus impressive: She got a scholarship to college, for example, and put herself through medical school; she grew up in rural Tennessee, where her parents still run a luncheonette.

I say, "She told you that?"

"Yeah," he says. "Why?"

"I don't think of psychiatrists talking about themselves too much."

It's not until he tells me that they're not in Freudian analysis and breaks out laughing that I realize he's not in analysis at all. Mary Pat is his new girlfriend.

He laughs like a madman, and I say, "Very funny," though it is, in fact, very funny just to hear Jack laugh, as well as a huge relief: Our father died not even two months ago.

My eggs and Jack's pancakes are set before us, and we stop talking to eat; we're at Homer's, the diner around the corner from his apartment in the Village.

I ask how he met Mary Pat.

He tells me, "Pete referred her."

For a moment he gets waylaid talking about the fishing shack he helped Pete restore this summer. Pete lives year-round on

Martha's Vineyard with his Newfoundland, Lila, who expresses her heartache by howling to Billie Holiday records: *Dog, you don't know the trouble I seen.*

Jack says Pete called when M.P. moved to town. "I think he's always been a little in love with her."

I say nothing; I have always been a little in love with Pete.

Though Jack didn't say he'd bring Mary Pat, I'm a little disappointed when he arrives at Homer's without her. "Just coffee," he says to the waiter.

He tells me that M.P. was mugged on her way home from work, and he was up half the night trying to calm her down.

"Jesus," I say, and ask where and when, and was there a weapon?

A knife; ten p.m.; a block from her apartment on Avenue D.

I say, "She lives on Avenue D?" D is for Drugs, D is for Danger, D is for Don't live on Avenue D unless you have to.

Jack says, "It's what she can afford."

I say, "I thought psychiatrists cleaned up."

"Maybe in private practice."

As Dr. Delmar, Mary Pat treats survivors of torture in a program at NYU Hospital.

From spending weeks at my father's bedside I have become alive to a level of pain I'd never known: Now I feel it on every street of Manhattan, in every column in the newspaper, and just the idea of someone who works to ease suffering eases mine.

I say, "When can I meet her?"

"Soon."

Sounding like a worried mother, I say, "She should take a cab when she works late."

"I know, but she says walking is her only exercise."

Jack is standing outside the White Horse Tavern when I arrive. He says, "Want to sit outside?"

It's November. "Why would I want to sit outside?"

He tells me that M.P. will; after spending all day in the hospital, she craves fresh air. He takes off his leather jacket and hands it to me, an act of chivalry in the name of Mary Pat.

I give in. "You love this girl."

He howls a mock forlorn "I do," imitating a country singer or Newfoundland.

We maneuver our legs under a picnic table; we are the sole outsiders, and Jack has to go inside to get the waitress.

We both order scotch for warmth.

Jack yawns and tells me that he and Mary Pat were up most of the night, discussing his new screenplay. He tells me that her notes were unbelievably smart, incredibly smart—smarter than his actual screenplay.

It occurs to me that I have never heard him more sure of any woman and less sure of himself. He catches sight of his dramaturge across the street, and I turn to look. She is tall and skinny in high heels. Her cheeks are flushed, and when she sees Jack she smiles, activating dimples.

Her hand is limp in mine, her voice shivery. "Pleased to meet you."

She kisses Jack full on the mouth and then says she thinks she's coming down with something; do we mind sitting inside?

Once we're seated, I pretend, as I always do with Jack's girlfriends, that I already like her: I tell her that I can hardly sit in high heels, let alone walk in them, and how does she do it?

She says, "I don't know."

Jack puts his hand across her forehead, and his eyebrows slant up in worry. "You have a fever."

"If you're sick," I say, "we can have dinner another night."

"No, no," she says. "I like a fever." Her smile is wan, her skin shiny. "You know, through the glass darkly."

I do not know; I'm not even sure I've heard her correctly. Her voice is so quiet I strain just for fragments.

We pick up our menus.

"I'm going to have a cheeseburger and fries," I say.

Jack says, "Same here."

Mary Pat says, "I don't think I can eat a whole one myself."

"You can share mine," he says.

"You don't mind?"

My brother, who usually slaps my hand if I take one of his fries, does not mind.

When our cheeseburgers arrive, Mary Pat ignores the extra plate brought for sharing, and eats right off Jack's. Instead of cutting the burger in half, she takes a bite and then he does. She even uses his napkin to wipe her mouth. I am reminded of the aid organization Doctors Without Borders.

"Jack told me that you met through Pete," I say.

"Oh, yes." She says, "He warned your brother about me," and the two of them seem to think this is funny.

I play along—ha, ha, ha: "What did he say?"

Jack asks Mary Pat, "What did he say?"

She says, "I'm trouble?" her voice so lush with sex, I think, *Hey, M.P., I'm right here, Jack's little sister, across the table.*

Her body reacts to the smallest shift in his; they are in constant bodily contact. She doesn't touch Jack directly, but rubs herself against him almost incidentally, like a cat. The one time he reaches for her hand, she lets him hold it for less than a minute. Then she takes it back and hides it in the dark under the table.

Maybe because of her whispery voice or her ethereal skinniness or her glass-darkly fever, Mary Pat gives the impression of not quite being here at the table, here at the White Horse, here on Earth. As though to assure myself of my own existence, I counter her quiet voice by raising mine, counter her little bites by taking big ones.

I try to talk to her, but it is just me asking questions and her answering them. My questions get longer, her answers shorter. Still I don't quit. I'm like a gambler who keeps thinking, *Maybe the next hand.*

The name of her parents' luncheonette? Delmar's.

The division of labor? Her father cooks; her mother serves.

If we were at Delmar's now, we'd order...? "Meat 'n' Two."

I say, "Meat and two?"

"One meat and two sides."

I love sides; I ask which are best.

"Butter beans," she says. "Grits, if you like grits."

I smile the smile of a grits liker, though not a single grit has ever entered my mouth. I say, "Did you hang out at the luncheonette a lot growing up?"

She nods.

I say, "Was it fun?"

"No," she says, making clear that she doesn't want to talk about this or to talk to me or to talk. She says, "Excuse me," and goes to the ladies' room.

"What?" I say to Jack.

He says, "She can't talk about her father."

"Were we talking about her father?"

When she returns, Jack puts his arm around her.

I say, "I didn't mean to pry."

Mary Pat says a wounded "Don't worry about it."

Jack does not call to ask what I think of Mary Pat, as he has with every other girlfriend he has ever introduced to me. He doesn't call at all.

When I call him, he is in bed with a fever of 103.

I offer to bring him soup, and he says that he has soup and juice and everything he needs—leftover from when he took care of Mary Pat.

A week later, when I call to ask if we're meeting at Homer's, he's still in bed.

He says that his fever is down. He just doesn't feel good.

I say, "What's the matter, Buddy?" our father's nickname for Jack.

"She hated my revision."

"What?"

"I told you she gave me notes on my script," he says. "She said I didn't understand anything."

I say, "You want me to come over?"

"Yeah," he says, and I do.

His night table is a mess of drugs—NyQuil, DayQuil, Sudafed, TheraFlu—a sticky dose cup, a mug, and a tea bag that looks like a mouse in rigor mortis. His bed is covered with screenplay pages and used Kleenexes, which, he says, are of equal value to Mary Pat.

"Does she know that your father died nine weeks ago?"

He says, "I asked her to be honest."

It takes me a minute to understand that he is defending her against me.

I clean up, I take his temperature, I make tea. I am stirring soup when Mary Pat calls, apparently contrite.

"She's coming over," Jack says, which means I'm supposed to go.

Jack arrives at Homer's, blurry with exhaustion and hobbling. He tells me that he's been working out. "I just overdid it." He says something indecipherable through a yawn, and, "... up really late."

I ask if he was working on his screenplay.

"No." He yawns. "We stayed up late, talking."

"Don't you babies ever sleep through the night?"

He says, "She was upset."

I think of the work that Mary Pat does and the stories she must hear every day.

"I woke up," Jack says, "and she was crying."

I nod in sympathy.

His voice is cloudy with sleep. "She kept telling me how sorry she was."

I say, "Why was she sorry?"

He seems suddenly to focus and to realize that he might not want to tell me this story. He hesitates before going on, but he does go on, too tired to obey his instincts. "She's still in love with her old boyfriend."

The words seem to spell out *The End,* and yet I don't hear *The End* in his voice or see *The End* in his face.

I say, "If she loves him so much, how come she broke up with him?"

I watch Jack try to remember. "She didn't feel she deserved to be happy back then."

What comes to mind is Jack's rendition of the Talking Heads' song which he changed from "Psycho Killer" to "Psycho Babble." I think of the refrain, *Run run run run run run run away.*

I say, "When didn't she deserve to be happy?"

"Her freshman year," he says. "He was a senior. Physics major. He played squash."

I'm confused. "So, she's been seeing him since her freshman year?"

"No."

"She ran into him?"

"No."

I say, "But she wants to get back together with him?"

"No," he says. "He's married with two kids. She doesn't even know where he lives."

It occurs to me that I might understand this story better if I were really, really tired.

My poor brother's eyes are tiny and his skin clam-colored; his hand trembles as he returns his coffee cup to the puddle in his saucer. He says, "The good thing is," and drifts off.

I say, "The good thing is..."

"She finally feels like she deserves to be happy."

Jack calls and says that he wishes he hadn't told me about M.P.'s old boyfriend.

I say, "I understand," and I do. There are things two people say in the middle of the night that don't make sense to a third at breakfast.

The next few times I ask, Jack tells me that Mary Pat is great, and then she is good, and then she is fine, and then she is okay.

Saturday night at four a.m. he calls me from her apartment. I know without asking that he is sitting in the dark; I can hear it in his voice.

"I blew it," he says.

I say, "I'm sure you didn't."

"I did," he says. "I blew it."

"How?"

"I just blew it," he says. "I blew it."

"Try to remember that we're having a conversation," I say, "and your goal is to impart information."

He says, "I should've proposed to her at the Boathouse." When I don't answer, he says, "In Central Park," as though to clarify. "That was the perfect moment."

I force myself to say the consoling words: "I'm sure you'll have another perfect moment."

"No," he says. "She said that was the perfect moment, and we can never get it back."

"Hold on there," I say. "You've known each other for like twenty minutes."

He doesn't answer, and I hear how irrelevant these words are to him. "Just bear with me," I say. "Forget about perfect moments for a minute. Do you really want *Mary Pat* to be your *wife*? You want *Mary Pat* to be the *mother of your children*?"

"Yes," he says.

I do not ask him if he thinks he would be happy with Mary Pat. Happiness, I realize, is beside the point. I realize, too, that he doesn't want me to help him figure anything out or to help him feel better. He wants me to help him win Mary Pat.

"Okay," I say. "Here's what I think you should do. Don't ask her to marry you. Give her room," I say. "Try not to need anything from her for a little while."

How can I tell that I have said something he wants to hear? The silence is just the same, but I know.

I imitate our father's calm authority: "We'll figure the rest out in the morning."

I've only called Pete a few times in my life, and as soon as I hear his hello, I remember why. He has settled in for the night, his feet by the fire, Dostoyevsky in hand, Lila's head on his lap; a phone call is breaking and entering.

We talk, but only about one percent of Pete comes to the phone. You get close to Pete by swimming or clamming or fishing, by weeding his garden, by singing while he plays guitar.

Every exchange is more strained than the last until I get to the emergency of my brother's love. When I finish, he says, "I don't think there's anything you can do, Soph." He is sympathetic but resolute, as though describing a house beyond restoration.

"You don't understand," I say. "I think he's going to propose to her."

He says, "They all propose."

For myself, I say, "Did you propose?"

He laughs. "No." It occurs to me that I have never known Pete to have a girlfriend.

"How are you?"

"You know," he says. "Okay."

"How's Lila?"

He says, "How are you, Lila?"

What I hear in the moment of quiet that follows is Martha's Vineyard in winter—the clouds in the sky, the wind on the beach, and the cold that stays on your clothes even inside.

Jack does not return my calls. I ask my mother if she's heard from him. She has. She says, "I can't wait to meet Mary Pat."

I know how hard my little brother is working, and I am reluctant to worry him. But when he asks me what I think of Mary Pat,

I tell him everything. "He's losing weight. He doesn't sleep anymore." It occurs to me this is how cults weaken the will of initiates.

Robert says, "It sounds like he's in love," and adds that the world's most coveted state is characterized by unrelieved insecurity and nearly constant pain.

The effect of his words is to remind me that it has been a long time since I have been in love.

"What about you?" Robert says. "Have you met anyone?"

He always asks, and I always have to say no, and I say no now. For the first time, he says he wants to introduce me to someone he knows, a pediatric heart surgeon.

"That's good," I say. "I have a pediatric heart."

He says, "Don't talk about my sister that way."

Before we hang up, I say, "Are you in love?"

"No," he says.

I ask if his wife knows.

"Of course," he says. "Naomi's the one who told me."

When Jack finally calls me, at work, he says, "Can you meet me?" instead of hello.

"When?"

He says, "Now."

Before I can ask where, he hangs up. Even though it's six p.m. on a weekday, I assume Homer's, and I'm right. Jack's at the counter, his head bowed. His face looks haggard, but his body surprisingly buff.

He says that he can't sleep or eat or think or write.

"Apparently you can work out, though."

"She won't call me back," he says.

I say, "I know how that feels."

He misses the jibe. "We had a fight."

"About what?"

"It wasn't really a fight." He tells the waiter, "Just coffee."

"He'll have pancakes and bacon with that." To Jack, I say, "Or do you want eggs?"

"I don't want anything."

I tell the waiter, "He'll have the pancakes."

Jack doesn't even seem to hear.

"You seem like you're in a coma," I say, and as soon as I say it, I feel sick. Our father was in a coma for days, and I have said *coma* the way people who don't know anything about it do, which is like calling out, *Can we get another coma over here?*

I say, "I meant stupor," but Jack is in such a stupor, he didn't even notice my coma.

When his pancakes come, he pushes the plate aside. He sighs, and sighs again. His voice is so quiet, it's as though he's talking to himself when he says, "I can't hit her."

"Sorry?"

"I can't hit her," he says, and I realize how tired and desperate he must be to say these words to me.

"And you want to hit her?"

He shrugs. "She wants me to."

"In bed," I say.

"Of course in bed," he says. "Where else?"

"Oh, I'm sorry," I say. "Of course, she wants you to hit her in bed. And you can't. Go on."

"She thinks it means I don't love her."

I say, "Can I hit her?"

"Sophie." His voice is a reprimand. "Her father used to beat her."

I think, *She probably deserved it,* but then I turn back into a human being. My brother's face is so tired and so sad it makes my face tired and sad. "Buddy." But even as I say, "If I were you, I'd try to get out of this thing," I know that nothing I say, no matter how wise or well put, will separate him from this woman.

He says, "It's not like I have a choice."

I say, "Of course you do."

"She's been seeing someone else," he says. "Some guy she works with."

I am about to say, *A victim?* But I correct myself in time: "A survivor?"

He defends Mary Pat even now: "She would never go out with a patient."

There are so many things I could say about Mary Pat. I could call her the one word you save for occasions such as this, the only sacred profanity. But my brother loves this woman, whoever she is, and deriding her would only deride him for loving her.

What else is there to say? I tell him that I've been editing a celebrity diet book at work. I say, "News flash: Eat less, exercise more."

When I slide the plate of pancakes in front of him, he says, "I'm not hungry."

"Do you think I care if you're hungry?" I say, "This has nothing to do with hunger. Hunger is beside the point. Hunger is a luxury you can't afford."

I pour syrup over the pancakes. When I cut into the stack, he says, dryly, "Leggo my eggo," repeating a commercial circa our childhood.

"You need a nap," I say.

He eats one bite, and then another.

While he finishes his pancakes, I plan the future. I will walk him home, and up the stairs to his apartment. He'll lie down. I'll shop for groceries. I will take him to a movie and out for dinner. In case my father is listening, I think, *We will look after each other.*

Mother

On any given day, Mother could have her pick of maids. The women, usually Hmong, would line the open markets and scurry after her, offering to carry her bags. Mother decided that she was going to plan a special meal. Father was coming home from the military soon. They would celebrate. The end of his absence, their reunion, the lunar new year. She would set an extra place at the table. She had just had a miscarriage. It was a bit crazy, she knew, but she was counting on Father to come and rescue her.

"Hello," a woman said. Mother stopped. The woman was toothless. Her hair was in a bun and greasy.

"My name is Tai," she said.

Mother noticed her thin cotton outfit. She was sweating.

"I need work. I'm good."

She had trouble in finding words but expressed herself in the simplest ways.

Mother removed her sunglasses. She was holding a dead chicken in her grip, and drops of blood were trickling down onto her foot. Mother reached into her market bag and handed Tai a *mangosteen*. "I remember," Mother said. "It was the only fruit worth eating in January."

Tai came home with her, and she carried Mother's dead chicken. The *mangosteen* would rot in just a day from a small puncture. She shuffled behind Mother by half a step. The two of them readied the house. The next morning, Tai went to the market alone. With nothing but more waiting, Mother took a bath. She remembered an incident when she was young, standing on a stool to peep into the kitchen window. A pile of sweets. Sweets her mother would never offer her. They were yellow. Dusty. She would eat them first before her two sisters and as many as possible. Her eyes too eager with a plan, she jumped off the stool and landed on a chick, killing it.

She did not think death, blood, pain, or make a sound. She

thought: I am going to get beaten. She scooped up the chick with her left sandal, ran to the well in the yard, and, in haste, tossed her sandal down into the well with the dead animal. They were her only pair, crusted, flat, barely performing. She could picture her mother seething: the missing sweets, the expense of new sandals. In haste again, she took her right sandal and threw it down the well also.

That was funny now. And she laughed in the tub. "When you laugh because no one is looking, you are well," she said.

Father never arrived for the dinner. He was not high up in the military ranks. When I was very young, I thought all men in uniform were important. And they are, I guess, but it did not mean that Father shot anyone or even ran for his life. He was under a much larger itinerary, and the most he would be told was what to do next. Sometimes, he would wait days for orders to come, and they would be simply to stay put. And then he would relay a telegram to Mother, and the illiterate Tai would hand her the news on yellow paper.

Father did return three weeks later, with a funny sore on his lip.

"A disease," Mother pronounced.

"Maybe he got it fighting," I said.

She rolled her eyes.

It was not hard for me to picture Mother horny, and she must have been. We all are, and nights are wasted trying to solve it. I was never afraid of thinking about my parents having sex. Men think about sex every forty-five seconds, and we are bound to run out of material if we do not include our relatives.

The next morning, Mother went to the market with Tai. She sat impatiently waiting for her, watching her run back and forth, in and out of the house. Mother had a strong sense for things wrong. She could smell it, and she knew if she waited long enough she would know what it was.

After washing her feet again and her sandals a second time, Tai finally appeared. She was nervous, Mother said, and she shuffled behind her all the way into Ben Thanh Market.

They made a daily purchase even though there was so much food left uneaten. A bag of rice, Mother wanted duck eggs. She sniffed an herb and rejected it. When I pictured Mother going to the market, I did not see it the way you might in the movies. No one screamed, she did not haggle, the prices were the prices. She turned down anyone who offered her anything more.

When they exited the market, a man in a cotton outfit was waiting for them. He was sweating. With not many teeth, he smiled at Mother. She became nervous. It was approaching wartime. Every Vietnamese woman started clutching her purse more often.

The maid's husband stared at us. When he tried to speak, he addressed the pebbles. The most amazing part of this story was that no one had to say anything to understand what was being proposed. Mother's maid had a husband. She wanted her husband to come and work with her. And so the three of them walked home as a group, the man carrying another dead chicken.

Tai often wore a white sweater, long arms that weighed her down. According to Mother, Tai and her husband ate the same meal for breakfast, lunch, and dinner—bloody raw fish with rice. It was disgusting. Mother could only watch before she taught her how to catch cockles with a colander from the waters nearby, and so for breakfast, lunch, and dinner, Tai ate cockles with rice. And this was what Mother needed in her life—loyalty. Her husband on one side, her servants on the other, like a set of parentheses. Safety. Outline. Shade. In the beginning, she followed Father from military base to military base through innumerable cities. But she hated living on the bases—the canned goods, the horrible radio, the endless round of cards, the war brides, the cafeteria lines. Even going to the bathroom felt bureaucratic. To make a dressing room for herself, Mother would ask her neighbor to close her eyes. Usually, the towns she got stuck in were ugly, with two seasons, wet and dry. No birds, where are the trees, what's that smell, a smothering sky. On a military base, nothing grows. Say their names aloud: Plei Ku, Da Nang, Can Tho, Saigon. Mother never had a real home.

When it was time to leave Viet Nam, many years later, it was night. I was six. For the third day in a row, I had rolled underneath Mother's bed in the middle of the night. I had been sleeping on the floor next to it. I only just remember this: a man, white, in camouflage yanked me out from underneath and put an oversized camouflage jacket on me. I have ever since hated camouflage. I was deposited out in front of our house. Tai stayed with me, her husband darted in and out of the house with Mother. I remember this, too: the sky was orange and the next-door neighbor was vomiting. Mother had one suitcase, packed with our belongings. A sleeve hung out of it like a piece of sandwich meat. Tai said goodbye to me. We hugged. Her husband whose name I never learned squeezed my arm. Then, Mother reached into her pocketbook and took out the key to our house and handed it to Tai. And in one moment, however brief, all the maids in Viet Nam owned everything. It was time to leave.

Refund

They had no contract. It would be a simple transaction. A sublet in Tribeca for the month of September. Two bedrooms and a terrace: $3,000.

They were almost forty years old, children of responsible, middle-class parents, and had created this mess out of their own sordid desires. Josh and Clarissa had lived for twelve years in a dingy brick high-rise in the Manhattan neighborhood of Tribeca. They had been lonely, met, married, worked at their art for years, presented their work to a world that was shockingly indifferent, floundered in debt, defaulted on student loans, began to lie to their parents about their financial status, and lived in a constant state of fear. They were afraid of what they might say when friends told them gleefully about their vacations; they were afraid of opening another magazine to find another grad school colleague profiled and beautifully photographed, modest, bemused; they were afraid of each other, disappointed that each could not rescue the other from this predicament of debt and bitterness. They lay in bed at 5:30 in the morning, listening to their three-year-old son, Sammy, hurtling toward the first sunbeam with the call: "More fun. More fun." The wistful, hopeful cry made their blood go cold. One of them stumbled towards the relentless dawn, inevitably tripping over the trucks that Sammy had lined up in hopeful parades, as though he still had the conviction that there was somewhere wonderful to go.

Their rent-subsidized apartment was located in a dull seventies high-rise, where, at first, they braved the abandoned, crumbling warehouses and hefty rats for a rent so cheap they could not afford to live anywhere else. But then the neighborhood changed. They were on the strip of land known as Tribeca, their building a few blocks south of Canal, six blocks north of the World Trade Center, and now there were lofts selling for twenty million dollars, new restaurants with glossy, slim customers posed as though in liquor ads, movie star neighbors moving in such rarified circles they were never actually seen. Walking into their own building, they heard shrill hallway arguments about the misbehavior of companion animals, feuds about laundry hoisted prematurely out of the dryer. The residents were on edge because they were doomed; the building would soon be privatized, rents hiked, and they would all end up on the street. Josh and Clarissa now skulked through their neighborhood with the cowed posture of trespassers.

Their son was almost three years old. Soon it would be time to send him to a preschool. In the park sandbox, mothers talked about Rainbows, the most expensive preschool in the area. Those who had been turned down or could not afford the school spoke of it with a strangled passion. One mother claimed she had stormed out when the director had asked to see her income tax statement during an interview. But another mother, whose son was a student there, leaned toward Clarissa one day after admiring Sammy's exuberant personality, and said, "That's the only place where they truly treat the children like human beings."

This statement had propelled Clarissa through the doors of Rainbows to observe a class. The director, dressed in flowing, silk robes, and with large, lidded eyes that made her resemble a woodlands creature from a fairy tale, walked Clarissa through the airy rooms. The director said that the children particularly enjoyed "Medieval Studies," which apparently meant that the children dressed up as kings and queens. Clarissa watched the children of successful lawyers, doctors, executives, and various moguls stack blocks, roll trucks, and cry. One child had tried to hand her a block. When she had smiled at him, a teacher gave her a laminated list of rules for class observation. Number 5 was: *Do not engage with a child who tries to talk to you. It interferes with their work.* She was ashamed that she had smiled at the child, and that shame convinced her that the school was the only place for Sammy to go.

"Ten thousand dollars," said Josh, "so that he can scribble? No. No. No." She mailed in the application, anyway—and when she received the acceptance she felt it was a sign of some greater good fortune. Their son gazed at them with his beautiful, pure brown eyes, his future gleaming, unsullied, new.

"At least visit the other schools," pleaded Josh, and she tried. At one, she peered through a square window in a door to see a crowd of children screaming to be let out. One child punched in a security code, a red light flashed, the door opened, and he shot out, to the roaring approval of the others. That was it. They had enough room on their Visa for the first tuition installment; they loaded it on.

Then Josh heard about a job for the two of them teaching art at a small university in Virginia, three weeks paid in September, accommodations for all of them in a hotel. They could hurl money toward Sammy's tuition. Their apartment would be empty for a month. It occurred to them they could sublet their apartment and pay off part of their substantial debt load. "Let's charge a fortune," said Josh.

Josh's college friend, Gary, an investment banker, delivered the subletter to them. "I think you can get three thousand," he said. Their rent was five hundred and fifty a month. Josh wrote the ad: *Fabulous Tribeca apartment. Two bedrooms, terrace. Three thousand for September.* Gary sent his friends a mass e-mail, and the call came the next day.

"My name is Kim. Gary gave me your name. He says you have apartment to let. I live in Montreal, and I am looking for accommodations in the city for September."

"Right," Clarissa said. "Thanks for calling. Well, we're by the Hudson, beautiful views, wood floors...uh...we have a dishwasher." She paused. "Down the block," she said carefully, "is Nobu."

"No-*bu*," said Kim, solemnly. There was silence. "I've known Gary for three years," Kim said. "We met in the south of France with his friends Janna from Paris and Juan from Brazil...we were in town for the day for the Beaujolais festival. We became friends. Now we follow the Michelin guide all over Europe together. We have a race to see who has the most frequent flyer miles...I have 67,000 but he has more." She paused. "I want to go to Nobu. I want to go with my friend Darla. She is my best friend. I want to walk there!"

"Now, it's not fancy," Clarissa said, alarmed.

"I want to walk to Montrachet!"

Kim wanted to send the money immediately; she magically wired $3,000 into their checking account, and that was that.

It was September 1. Kim held the keys to their apartment. They checked their ATM as they headed out of town. The three thousand dollars registered on their account. Josh whistled when he saw it. They drove toward a month's employment, a couple in front, a child in the car seat, across the bridges, out of the city. She and Josh held hands. Clarissa turned once to look back at the city, the skyline rising, glittering, frozen and grand in the clear autumn light.

She had dropped Josh off to look at televisions at a department store when she heard the news on the car radio. Her body startled. Howard Stern's show came on the air, and the tone of the hosts was terrifying: lost and humorless. "We know who did it," said a caller, "and we need to go kill them."

Her hands were trembling so it was difficult to grip the wheel. She raced to the store, where the staff and customers had abandoned their personas and stood, statues, in front of the television screens.

She stood with the group in the electronics section, in front of dozens of screens. They saw the Towers on fire. A giant tower buckled on the screen in front of them, frail as a sandcastle. Grown men around her yelled, No! in shocked, womanly voices. Sammy was immediately attracted to the picture. "Booming sound," said their son. She let him watch. "Booming!" he yelled.

The fact that they lived by the Trade Center made them objects of concern. "I'm so sorry," said strangers. They stood, awkward, marked with an awful, bewildering luck. "Where would you have been?" asked someone eagerly, as though they had been potential victims and they craved an intimacy with the disaster. "We would have been one block away," Clarissa said. Her arms became cold. This admission felt strangely like bragging. It occurred to her that others thought that they could have been dead. Around nine o'clock they would have been steps away, bringing Sammy to his first day of school.

The chair of the art department told them to take the day off, and they spent it in the hotel. It was stale and hot, full of a thousand strangers' breaths. She was not supposed to be here, and did not know what to do with herself, grubby, ashamed, alive. She felt fat and sickened by her own flesh. The TV droned casualty estimates into the room. The curtains were drawn, and the room was dark. They tried all day to get Sammy to nap. He popped out of his room, awake, excited by their fear. He imitated them, shouting into the phone. "Hello!" he called gaily. "Hello."

Somehow, the day ended. They drove down the dark streets, Sammy screaming with exhaustion, until he fell asleep. A student had said to them: Providence had brought them here. "You have been blessed," the student said in a respectful tone, before inviting them to church. Clarissa declined, though she kept thinking about this. She asked Josh, "Do you think we were blessed?"

"We're not special," he said. "Don't feel special. It could be us next time. It could be us any minute."

She looked out the window. This was not the answer she wanted. "Why do you say that?" she said. "How do you wake up in the morning? How are you going to walk Sammy across the street—"

He reached for her hand. They were ridiculous with unexpected luck. His fingers felt strange, rubbery; she clung to them, bewildered by the raw facts of their fingers, their hair.

"Hello," said the voice, aggrieved, three days later. "Hello, Clarissa. It's me."

"Hello?" asked Clarissa. "Who is this?"

"I was on my way there. I wanted to go to the observation deck. I went the wrong way on the subway, or I would be dead. I got out, and there were all these people running. Then I saw the second plane. I started running, and then I couldn't get the windows closed because I've never seen windows like yours—"

"I'm sorry," Clarissa whispered, "I'm sorry—"

"They said there's a bomb under the George Washington Bridge!" Kim shouted. "I can't get the ferry to New Jersey, it's closed. Is there a heliport in Manhattan? I'll pay anything to get to a heliport. Can you tell me?"

"I don't know," said Clarissa. "I don't know where one is—"

There was a pause. "I'm leaving town," said Kim. "I can't stay here. And I want a refund. I want it all back."

One day before they left Virginia to return to New York, Clarissa received an e-mail: IN REGARDS TO REFUND

I have not heard from you in regards to the status of my refund. Perhaps you are too busy to think about me now. All the hotels are giving refunds. Also free rooms in the future, suite upgrades. My pet peeves are injustice and dishonesty. I know when I am being treated fairly. You did not tell me certain facts about the apartment, which was, I am sorry to say, filthy. Black goo all over the refrigerator. I had to wear plastic gloves to keep my hands clean.

Darla and I planned our vacation for a long time. We are best friends. We were going to buy the same clothes, go to the newest restaurants. People would admire us and say who are those glamour girls. Her hair is red and more beautiful, but I will admit I have nicer legs, we wanted to start a commotion.

I expect to receive payment of US$3000 within a week.

When they got out of their cab at Canal Street, the border between civilian New York and the war zone, they unloaded their luggage by the rows of blue police barricades. "Let's see your ID," said the state trooper, standing, trim and noble in his brown uniform, surrounded by pans of homemade cookies. "Do you live here, or do you have reservations?"

They looked at him.

"The restaurants gave us lists of people who have reservations," he said, pulling out a piece of paper. They offered their driver's license, and the officer agreed: this was where they lived.

He offered to give them a ride to their building. The car floated by the gray, scrolled buildings, the streets deserted as though the neighborhood had simply been a stage set, built quickly, then abandoned. The sky had become a pale, sickly orange and gray. There were too many police cars posed at corners; sirens pierced the warm air. There were American flags everywhere, as though everyone was desperate to have the same thought. People hurried down the streets, carrying groceries, pushing strollers; some were wearing surgical masks. She was suddenly leaden with sadness, a feeling that was precious in its simplicity.

Kim had left in great haste, sheets piled in the living room, a pale lipstick in the bathroom sink. Clarissa picked up the lipstick and touched the tip; the color was an unearthly pink. Sammy ran ahead of them. She thought that they should make some grand entrance, that they should say something profound to each other, but she merely listened to their presence ring through the apartment; the sound was perplexingly beautiful.

They were home. There was the smell, unlike anything she had smelled before. Burning concrete and computers and office car-

pets and jets and steel girders and people. There was nothing natural about the smell, it tasted bitter and metal in her mouth, and
blew through their neighborhood at variable times; the mornings
began, sweet and deceptive, the afternoons became heavy with it.
She began to get a sore throat, and her tongue became numb. The
girls at the American Lung Association table gave her a white
paper mask and told her that there was nothing to worry about,
but to keep her windows closed and stay inside. She walked
against the small stream of people wearing paper masks. The
streets were dark and shiny, the sanitation trucks spraying down
the street to keep the dust from lifting into the air. A man walked
the streets in a suit and a gas mask. Did he know something they
did not? Where did he get the gas mask? People used to strut in
their neighborhood, but now everyone was simply moving forward, in dull impersonations of themselves.

She went out to the market the first morning after they
returned. She pushed Sammy in his stroller downtown, heading
straight toward the empty sky. In the market, she picked out cereal, detergent, apples to the pop soundtrack in the supermarket,
the cheerful music that usually made her feel as though she were
part of some drama greater than herself. Now it floated around
her, impossible, but the supermarket did not shut it off.

When she ran into neighbors, anyone: Modesto, the mainte-
nance men in the building, the counter man at the bodega, mothers from the playground, she moved toward them, the fact of
their existence, her fingers like talons. It did not matter that she
did not know their names. How are you, they asked each other,
and it seemed like they were saying I love you.

"How are you?" Modesto asked.

"Where were you?" she asked.

"How is your apartment?"

"I'm glad to see you."

The meetings were hushed and tender, and then, with further
discussion, she found that the neighbors had become deformed
by a part of their personalities. The mothers who had been angry
now were enormous, stiff-shouldered with anger, the mothers
who were fearful were feathery, barely rooted to the ground.
"Why do they close the park for asbestos," said one angrily, "when
before it was just full of piss and shit."

She stood with Josh, that first week, looking out their closed window at the lines of dump trucks taking the rubble to the barge. They sat, sweaty, greasy, in their living room, listening to the crash of the crumbled buildings as they fell into the steel barge. The swerve of the cranes sounded like huge, screaming cats, and when the heavy debris crashed into the barge, the sound was so loud they could feel it in their jaws.

They drifted quickly from their damp new gratitude for their lives to the fact that they had to live them. One week after their return, they sat beside the pile of bills that had accumulated. They sat before the pile as though before a dozen accusations; then Josh got up from the pile of bills that they could not pay. He went to his closet and brought out suits that she had not seen since he was in his twenties. She was startled when she saw him, the same slim figure, but now with gray hair. This sudden aging seemed a terrible betrayal. Suddenly, she realized that she had stopped looking closely at herself in the mirror. She dragged out some of the dresses she had worn fifteen years ago: stretchy Lycra dresses that clung to her skin. Now she looked like a sausage exploding from its casing. She had been hostage to the absurd notion that by acting young, you will not age. The part-time jobs, the haphazard routine, had kept them mired in a state of hope, preserved at the crest of some wonderful transformation.

"We were fools," he said.

Clarissa looked at herself in the mirror. She tried to hold her stomach in.

"We have to get real jobs. We should have had them fifteen years ago. What are we doing?"

"What about your art?" she asked. "We can cut back. We can eat beans more." He stared at her. "We can get another gallery, you're doing great work—"

She hated the tinny, rotting optimism in her voice. It had pushed them forward blindly, roughly, toward an imagined place where they would be seen for who they really were. She had wanted to walk through museums to see her work displayed on the walls. That sort of presence would, she had thought, cure her sorrow for her own death. But of course, it would not.

"We were idiots," he said.

They looked out the window at the smoke rising. His eyelashes were dark and beautiful. She remembered how when she married him, she hoped that their children would have those eyelashes, believed that loveliness would be protection against some cruelty. She rubbed her face, which was damp with sweat. Her mind seemed to have stopped. There was a short pause outside; the crane operators stopped for a moment of silence whenever they found part of a body. She looked out and saw one of the workers holding his hat. She opened one of the windows. The sickening, metallic smell entered the apartment.

"Kim wants all her money back," she said.

He lifted his hands in bewilderment.

"I'd give it back," she said. "Of course I would. But the way she yelled at me, and how she said this place was dirty where I know it was clean—"

"How can we pay her?" he laughed bitterly. "We can't pay anyone."

Dear Kim:

We are so sorry for your terrible experience. We are so glad you were not harmed. This is indeed a terrible time for the world. You did stay in our apartment for ten nights, and I have calculated this stay, at current hotel rates, at $150 a night. We are also deducting a fee for cleaning the apartment, as you did leave a window open letting some contaminated dust inside. This leaves you with a refund of $1,000. The first installment of this, in $20, will arrive in a week. Peace be with you.

She took a deep breath and pressed "Send."

She took Sammy to his first day of school. She walked down the street, past the taped fliers. The local day spa was offering free massages for firemen and policemen. A neighborhood restaurant offered a $25 Prix Fixe, Macaroni and Roast Beef, Eat American. Donations to Ladder 8 for Missing Fireman accepted. Dozens of Xeroxed faces of the missing clung to lampposts, wrapped with tape; they stared into the street. Loving husband and father. Our dear daughter. Worked on the 87th floor. Worked at Windows on the World. Please call. She walked by them slowly, and suddenly she could not breathe. The missing people were on every corner. They were smiling and happy in the photos, and many were younger than her.

The preschool was a block north of the wooden blue police barricades that separated regular life from the crumbled heap of buildings, the endless black smoke. Her stroller rattled past them and through the doors of the preschool. The school staff floated around, greeting everyone, with an unnerving intimacy, by their first names. Sammy darted into his classroom, and she stood with a cloud of mothers. They had walked to school under the smoky, foul skies, wearing leather coats in blue and orange. It seemed a paltry, mean decision, deciding what to wear, waking up and hearing the broken buildings falling into the boats. They had decided to dress up. Their hair was frosted golden and brown, and they were beautiful, and when they left, they cupped hands over their mouths.

"Have you gone out to dinner yet?" she heard one mother ask another. "You wouldn't believe the good deals down here, plus you can get reservations. Prix fixe at Chanterelle, thirty-five bucks, incredible, plus you have money for a good bottle of wine."

"The Independence has a special, Eat American," said another. "The wait staff is fast and gracious. They have the most exquisite apple pie."

Clarissa closed her eyes and rubbed her face, wondering whether she should admire these mothers' resilience or be appalled.

"We were refugees at the Plaza," she heard another mother say. "They had a special for everyone living below Canal. We had to go. They were generous. Our place was covered in that dust. We started throwing up, and I knew we had to get out. It cost a ton to get it cleaned. Should we stay or go? Can someone just tell me?" She whirled around, looking.

The teacher came over. "The children are doing well," he said. "Do you want to say bye before you go?"

Now Clarissa swerved through the room like a drunken person. Your child was not in the world, and then he was, suddenly, part of it. She crouched and breathed his clean, heartbreaking smell. "I'm going bye," she said.

Her child ignored her. Slowly, she stood up.

In the office off the main hallway, the in-house psychologist was holding a drop-in support session in which parents could talk about their feelings about sending their children to preschool three blocks from the site. Clarissa stood with the group clustered around the psychologist. One mother said, "My child screamed the whole way here, saying she was scared and didn't want to go, and I dropped her off, but then, well, I wonder, is she right to be scared?"

"Why is she right?" asked the psychologist.

"Well, because," called Clarissa, from the back.

"You have to believe it is safe," said the psychologist. "You tell them a kid's job is to go to school, and a parent's job is to keep you safe."

"But what if we don't know if it's safe?" Clarissa asked.

"Where is it safe?" the psychologist said. "Here? Brooklyn? Vermont? Milwaukee?"

The parents leaned toward her, awaiting an answer.

"You have to tell them a little lie," the psychologist said.

Later that day she received an e-mail with the heading: STUNNED.

> I don't know how you decided on this number as a refund. It is very unfair. Who are you to decide how much money to refund me? You were lucky; I was the one who suffered. I was on my way there!
>
> You did not tell me about the low water pressure or the scribbled crayon on the walls. Those facts would have made me not rent the apartment, and then I would NOT have been there. I thought you were my friend. Some friend. Do you even know what a friend is? Darla, my best friend, is kind to everyone, especially kittens. She once went to the animal shelter and brought her old Gucci towels to make the kittens more comfortable. I could see the fat attendants eyeing them! She told them to make sure the kittens took their towels with them to their new home.
>
> You left oily hairs in your hairbrush. I have your hairbrush. I have your Maybelline mascara. It is a horrid color. Who would put Maybelline on her eyelashes? Who would look good in navy blue? Are you trying to be younger than your age? You do not look so youthful in the snapshots on your refrigerator. You dress as though you think you are. You should not wear jeans when you are in your late thirties. I don't care if it is a bohemian sort of thing, it is just sad.
>
> I am requesting $3000 plus $1000 for every nightmare I have

had since the attack, which currently totals 24. You owe me US$27000, payable now.

Josh found a job as an illustrator at an advertising firm, and each morning, he sprinted down their hallway toward the office that gave him a new life. Sammy would not say goodbye without giving his father one of his toys to keep during the day. "Take one toy," Sammy said, thrusting a tiny plastic dinosaur or little truck into the pocket of his father's suit. Sammy could not decide which toy he wanted his father to have to remember him, and when Josh finally had to leave, Sammy began to wail. He began to race after his father, and she had to grab him. "Daddy will be back," she said in a strained, cooing voice. "We'll see him later—"

He looked at her as though she were a fool.

One morning she tried to distract him by walking up to SoHo to see which artists had shows up. She peered at one, where one member of the staff had expressed interest in her work, but had then vanished in an abrupt, unexplained departure. Another young woman, perhaps ten feet tall, wearing the monochrome dark outfits all the gallery staff wore, came over. Sammy was butting his head against the doorway, like a small bull.

"I'm sorry, but he can't come in," she said.

Her face was perfectly blank, which Clarissa wanted to see as a personality deficiency, but was instead an adaptive expression to New York and the desperate artists that banged on this gallery's door. Sammy lurched forward. The girl blocked the door. "Sorry," she said, sounding strained, "ma'am—"

Clarissa grabbed Sammy. She bumped into the American flag that was hanging from the gallery's door.

"God bless America," said the girl, quickly. They loved all of America, but they were afraid of her.

"Come on," she said to Sammy. "I'll get you a ball."

She bought him a small red ball, and they passed the local park where they had spent much of their time before the attack. It had been beautiful, children playing under large green trees, honeyed patches of sunlight. Now the plants in the garden had been flattened when people raced, terrified, out of the park. The park had been closed briefly to clean up asbestos contamination. Sammy hurled his new ball into the park and darted in, chortling with joy. His ball was rolling to a garbage bin that said, NO PLAYING ON OR AROUND THIS CONTAINER. On the trees were fliers: EPA IS LYING. TOXIC DUST EVERYWHERE. UNITE!

"No!" she yelled. "No more ball."

She grabbed him by the waist and lifted him. He scratched her, leaving two red lines on her arms. He kicked. She struggled to find a way to hold him so that he would not hurt her, but he was wild. She wanted to scream at him, but instead whispered shut up into the air. She was not a good mother, she was afraid. "Come on," she yelled, and swung him up on the shoulder. His scream vibrated through his Elmo shirt. She hated him for revealing to her what a terrible mother she was. She did not know how to protect him from the world. When he was older, he would not remember the Towers. She envied his ignorance, longed for it.

"Hey!" someone called. It was a kindly park janitor. "I got your ball for you," she said.

"It was by that bin, you're not supposed to touch it—"

The janitor looked at her. "You can just wipe it off." She took a Kleenex from her pocket and wiped the ball. Clarissa wondered what sort of person would live with their child by a toxic zone, beside police barricades encircling targets of violence. She shuddered, for that sort of person was herself.

"That's just where they keep the rat poison," said the janitor, cheerfully.

"The rat poison," said Clarissa, numbly. She had never thought the term rat poison would sound nostalgic, but she was strangely calmed.

Dear Clarissa:

You have forgotten about me. I have not forgotten about you. You were lucky. You were out of town. I had to endure your apartment. I can still feel the dirt on my skin. I cannot believe that you keep a child in that filthy apartment. You cannot control him from drawing on the walls. Furthermore, his drawings do not even show any artistic merit.

This is a pathetic way for someone who is 38 to live. I figured it out. I have ten more years of life to live over you. Ha ha! This is how I wanted to spend it: wake up, go to the top of the building, look out and take pictures with my new camera, come down, go to lunch at Nobu, walk around SoHo, buy something for my husband, go look at the shoes at Prada, have tea at the Plaza, jet off to Zermatt, stop in London. I want it all. I have the good taste to appreciate what is worthy in life.

My refund is US$29,000, payable now.

Dear Kim:

Don't try to pass the buck to me. You lived. You were lucky. Do you know what we were doing when you were here trying all the restaurants? Working. We are always working. We never rest. Do you know how many jobs I've had in the last year, trying to make money and make time for my art? Twelve. Do you know how close I came to getting a review in the Times? The guy came and loved my work. The words he used were "ground-breaking." Then along came this woman who videoed her own vagina and played the video to the soundtrack of The Sound of Music. There was room for just one review and she got it. It was a good one.

I am considering the refund and the appropriate amount considering the fact that we should all rise above ourselves during this terrible time. Peace be with you.

Each morning, when she walked Sammy into Rainbows, she felt first a sweet, exquisite rush of relief. Sammy jumped out of the stroller to a cream-colored room scented like oranges, inconceivably sweet. "Hello, Sammy," the teachers said, as though he was a visiting dignitary. "Sammy's here. Hello, Sammy. Hello."

They allowed him into this beautiful room, and waved at her, expecting her to walk out to continue her own life. She looked at the street, and she did not know where she could go. The hallway was mostly empty. She sat and watched the children play.

The mother who had been a refugee at the Plaza was heading a committee to raise money for tuition lost when parents withdrew their children. She was taking a poll in the hallway regarding how much to charge for the tickets. "I'm thinking something spectacular. A French theme," she told Clarissa. "Dinner, casino, a silent auction. Do you think people would pay fifty, one hundred, or two hundred per ticket?"

"I would pay one thousand," Clarissa said.

The woman looked right at her. It was as though Clarissa had told her something wonderful about herself. "Yes," she said, softly.

Dear Clarissa:

It is not my concern that you never rest. You cannot get the money from me. It was your choice to pursue this "job" of artist. Why would I owe you anything? You were not honest with me. Honesty is the best policy. When Darla left her husband, she told him that she could not stand his skinny legs. That was just something she felt he should know. We all have our tolerances. The knowledge might have helped him in his later dating life. You should have told me about the water pressure, scribbled crayon, hallway odor, broken TV, useless air conditioner. Why didn't you? I expect US$31,000 payable now.

Dear Kim:

You idiot. You have been spared. Other people died who were nicer than you. Do you even know how to love?

Dear Clarissa:

How dare you. I was there. You were not. I ran. I almost lost my life, so you have lost your right to harass me. How dare you ask if I can love. I love many people. I love friends. I love good service in restaurants. I love people who bring me delicious things. I love the crème brûlée at the Four Seasons. I love the shoe salesgirl at Bendel's. So you see I have a great ability for love. Maybe you could learn something about it. Love! Love! Love!

You owe me US$31,000, payable now.

There were no more e-mails. At night, Clarissa lay beside Josh, awake, listening to the wild screaming of the cranes.

On October 30, she sat down and wrote a check for two hundred and sixty-three dollars and seventy-five cents. There was no reason for this amount except that it was what they had left in the bank account that month. She did not know what to write on the note, so she scribbled, quickly: *Here is your refund. God Bless.*

Halloween would be Sammy's last day at the school. The bad tuition check for $2,000 had been sent a week before, and she wanted to stop showing up before they could ask her about it. Sammy dressed as a lion. All the children were in costume. A few mothers were loitering in the lobby, captivated by the sight of their children pretending to be something else. Sammy's class was populated with two miniature Annies, a Superman, a ballerina, three princesses, some indeterminate sparkly beings, a dog, and Sammy, the lion. The teacher read them a Halloween story, speaking to them as though she believed they would live forever. The children listened as though they believed this, too. Clarissa pressed her hands to the glass window that separated the parents from their children; she wanted to fall into the classroom and join them.

After school, she wanted to buy Sammy a special treat. She bought him a blue helium balloon at a party store. He marched down the street, grinning; she lumbered after him, this tiny being with a golden mane and tail. Suddenly, Sammy stopped and handed her the balloon. "Let it fly away," he said.

"I'm not getting you another," she said.

"Let it fly away!" he shouted. "Let it!"

She took the balloon and released it. The wind pushed it roughly into the air. Her son laughed, an impossibly bright, flute-like sound. Other people stopped and watched the balloon jab into the air. They laughed at Sammy's amusement, as though captivated by some tender memory of themselves. Then the balloon was gone.

"Where is it?" he asked.

"I don't know," she said.

Her child looked at her.

"Get it," he said.

A week later, she picked up the phone. "Two hundred and sixty-three? How did you come up with this number? You owe me $54,200, why don't you give me my money?"

"Look!" said Clarissa. "You went the wrong way on the subway. Why do you keep bothering us?"

"You were lucky," said Kim. "You weren't where you were supposed to be."

"You weren't, either," said Clarissa. "You went the wrong way—"

"Maybe it wasn't the wrong way. Maybe the Towers were the mistake. Why would I have wanted to go there, anyway? Maybe I was supposed to meet someone there, and they never showed up. What do you think of that?"

Clarissa felt cold. "Were you supposed to meet someone there?"

"Would I get my $54,200?"

"Were you meeting someone there?" asked Clarissa. "Were you?"

"She is named Darla," said Kim.

"Why didn't you say this?" asked Clarissa.

"Will you pay me my money?"

Clarissa's throat felt hot.

"I was talking to her on my cellphone," said Kim. "She was on the elevator to the observation deck." She paused. "She wanted to go to the Empire State Building, but I thought at the Towers we would get a better view."

What did one owe for being alive? What was the right way to breathe, to taste a strawberry, to love?

"Kim," said Clarissa, "I—"

"Do you know how long I'm going to charge you?" Kim said, her voice rising.

Clarissa closed her eyes.

"Do you know?" asked Kim.

BOB HICOK

Solstice: voyeur

I watched the young couple walk into the tall grass and close
the door of summer behind them, their heads floating
on the golden tips, on waves that flock and break like starlings
changing their minds in the middle of changing their minds,
I saw their hips lay down inside those birds, inside the day
of shy midnight, they kissed like waterfalls, like stones
that have traveled a million years to touch, and emerged
hybrid, some of her lips in his words, all of his fists
opened by trust like morning glories, and I smelled green
pouring out of trees into grass, grass into below, I stood
on the moment the earth changes its mind about the sun,
when hiding begins, and raised my hand from the hill
into the shadows behind the lovers, and contemplated
their going with my skin, and listened to the grass
in wind call us home like our mothers before dark.

AL HUDGINS

Drum

He lunged for the shut-off switch when he heard the scream.
But the brutal five-inch teeth on the rotating drum,
designed to excavate the coal face, had already destroyed

helmet and hair, scalp and brain. Its rotation
diminishing now, the carbide-tipped cutter bits
dripping with the miner's mistake. The noise declining

as the massive drum, about six feet long, rolled
to a stop and fell silent. The machine's remaining motors
droning dirges now. This coal seam had a name,

the coal mine, too, and even the continuous miner,
run by remote controls hung from the neck,
was identified with engraved letters on its scarred metal skin.

But this other name they knew they'd never say again
as casually as they'd done only moments before.
No one wanted to aim his headlamp there.

No one wanted to speak his name out loud.
He shouldn't have been there. It shouldn't have happened.
The rest of the section turned as one to the foreman

who approached the shadowed cavity deep in the coal face,
bowing his head to bring his light to the edge
slowly, the beam casting severe shadows

on the black ridges of coal, alien as rocks
lit by stark sunlight on the surface of the moon,
seen from the window of a passing capsule.

Behind the men standing numb, the feeder belt
snaked out empty to the surface, alerting
the superintendent there, then slid on back

beneath the clattering pulleys, to where it began,
its echoing percussion pounding their hearts like pickaxes,
the grim business of reclaiming the dead already underway.

Visible Masses of Condensed Vapor Song, Scotland

They're going to Glasgow, they're going to Inverness
    and to Skye. They'll ride over bogs of musk ox
and arctic foxes, tracing the scat of polar bears,
    open-mouthed masses swallowing snatches of blue vacancies,
ragged absences filling the empty air,
    sea birds climbing, vanishing
only to emerge in Reykjavík and west, soaring
    over the frozen moss, sponge, scrub, and footprints of an Inuit
at the aerodrome as he lifts off in his Cessna, later
    revving the snowmobile, toting the mobile phone,
checking out the overcast, his head filled
    with schemes for studying weather in Nunavut, north of
Baffin Bay, how to track highs and lows in masses
    of speeding clouds, calling back the song of grandfather's
huskies pulling sleds over vast acres of snow.

Blue Dementia

In the days when a man
would hold a swarm of words
inside his belly, nestled
against his spleen, singing.

In the days of nightriders
when life tongued a reed
till blues & sorrow songs
called out of the deep night:
Another man done gone.
Another man done gone.

In the days when one could lose oneself
all up inside love that way,
& then moan on the bone
till the gods cry out in someone's sleep.

Today,
already I've seen three dark-skinned men
discussing the weather with demons
& angels, gazing up at the clouds
& squinting down into iron grates
along the fast streets of luminous encounters.
I double-check my reflection in plate glass
& wonder, Am I passing another
Lucky Thompson or Marion Brown
cornered by a blue dementia,
another dark-skinned man
who woke up dreaming one morning
& then walked out of himself
dreaming? Did this one dare
to step on a crack in the sidewalk,

to turn a midnight corner & never come back
whole, or did he try to stare down a look
that shoved a blade into his heart?
I mean, I also know something
about nightriders & catgut. Yeah,
Honey, I know something about talking with ghosts.

Ode to the Guitar

for Flavio

The plucked strings tremble
& traverse the heart,
back through that other
strong muscle singing blood
& guilt. Press a finger down
& the message changes into blame
& beauty, into the scent of a garden
rising from peat moss & brimstone...
the frets & shaped neck worked
& caressed into a phantom limb
of hope. Does it have anything to do
with how the player's shoulder blades
curve out as if bowing over an altar
or how the doors of day & night
have been flung open, made to bridge
differences? Chance is fretted
till love moans swell in a gourd
hanging on an unknotted vine.
The strings hum inside stone,
undoing all the bright hooks
of promise stitched into silk
& printed cloth. Each note
true as a bone turning to dust,
suspended like an old belief
blooming from hush & blues
cries on the horizon. Catgut
& wood breathe together till
there's a beckoning of gold
left quivering in the dark.

Deception

Has a glow to it, distant and round at the end of the mine
shaft, a yellow malignant light.

Once seen, it loses power, becomes tarnished and dull
as river stones, lifted from their affair with water.

Money that has lain too long in the vault no longer has value.
The currencies we so believed in have changed.

To build the secret cell ultimately will involve torture.
One forgets where one has come from, one's companions.

Announces itself with the loud cacophony of trapped birds,
intercepted en route to their illegal sale.

There is a truth in it, which is suffocating, buried somewhere
alive. There is the dress left un-hemmed, drain field sinking.

One wants to believe in a strong voice, the snare
the earth caves into, the stinking pool of rotting timbers, sod.

The din is the din of I did not choose this.
Though one is left fingering the beads of deception in the dark.

Deception holds us sweetly while it carves with a dull knife.
Then the dreams begin so even sleep is unsafe for us.

Deception has a partner, sometimes a twin, whose face
turns away from us. Whose hair is an unnatural shade of red.

They are experts in erasure, transforming words into a story
we all want to believe: one that isn't anyone else's business.

Deception swallows all other points of view, and hence,
there are no lies. Blind-side. Hoodwink. Always a catch.

All that we banked on slid into the stream during the rains.
Silt, that solidity a deception. A lover turns an ugly face toward us.

And the deceived? She is losing her feathers. She has eaten
her foot. She exists with the ghost-letters, the forgotten language.

ADRIAN C. LOUIS

April in Oglala

Here where I have driven
past a thousand times,
here off the two-lane
blacktop, the tattered
blanket of April tries
to warm the icy lies
and whys of what lies
a few feet beneath
the surface of what we know.
A loud, yellow backhoe
and several diggers delve
into the hardened breasts
of our mother earth
and extract a spirit.
The spirit smiles briefly
at the mix of sun and sadness.
Somewhere someone sings:
In the sweet by and by,
We shall meet on that beautiful shore.
One spirit is going home, away
from this dark, violent, red land.

The Glue Trap

The long-tailed mouse that gnawed
a hemisphere into my box of ginger snaps,
the dust-gray mouse whose dung
speckled the kitchen floor and countertop,
the mold-puff mouse whose claws
roamed through paper garbage bags,
creaking crumpled cellophane,
the pointy-nosed mouse with nostrils trembling,
the defenseless-eyed mouse, cute and sad-eyed,
shocked by sudden light,
the chomping, big-footed mouse that evoked
longer-toothed rodent relations,
the heaving, golf-ball fat mouse
that planned to run on felt-tip toes to digest,
to sleep in his jagged hole in the wall,
has stepped into the glue trap
and spent the night defecating, squirming,
feet stuck, knees unable to unleash,
so it can only rock desperately,
taking dream-lunges into the home
it will never enter again.

This condemned, filth-fuzzy tear,
this handball of breath, whose exhausted snout
rested on glue for once and forever,
squeaks in my kitchen cabinet
so I, now glued to its dilemma,
must recall its tiny rolled feces,
the disgust it sowed in my food,
the half-moon signature of its gnaw,
the nightly invasion of its hunger,
and forget completely the innocence of its hunger
trapped in my invasion of its life,

deserving to be snuffed out mercifully,
crushed by a mallet, or well-poisoned,
or coldly dropped into boiling water
rather than be left to suffer for days,
grasping for food and the freedom of swift legs.
But I have no mallet or poison,
nor the stomach to boil it
and smell its cooked odor,
no way to ennoble my animal role:
my paw hurls the shredded prey
deep into buzzing forest
where second by second its squeak dissolves into the cosmos,
day's wind, night's rustle, and the ancient hunger of insects.

A Principle of Perspective

Call it the distance at which certain universals quiver into focus.
Call it a kind of motif in the face, a relief in recognition, a
cathartic thrill from the comfort of a couch. It's why a Russian
can write of slow death, and an American can feel his scrotum
tighten as he reads the tale—even in translation—then walk away
refreshed. And it allows an Englishman to write of love and loss,
and for a boy in Iowa to read those words and feel he knows that
courtier's life though of his own he don't know shit—verily, not
even the teat in his hand that fills the foaming bucket up. He's far
too close, and that's the point. But add perspective and it comes:

It's a clear morning, and the chores are underway. In the feedlot
some border has been crossed, and a son stands face to face with
his father—at the distance no human voice can bridge, the
distance at which lovers whisper promises. Something in their
stance is wrong, too still, too tense. It's hard to read precisely
what it is that sends his mother running from the hen house, her
apron full of eggs. She has seen it come to this before, the son
knocked down by the father who stands there as the boy learns
how to crawl again. But today it is the son who stands. He has
broken the vessel of his father's face and released the secret
hidden there behind the hate, the grim slate on which he tallies
up his losses to the world. On hands and knees in hoof-scarred
dirt, the father searches for the breath driven from his lungs by a
punch the son has telegraphed for years—each time his welling
words were bitten back, each time he had to pay for something
that he did or didn't do. Perhaps in time he will construe the way
the Herefords waited patiently, expecting hay that he would
never give again, how he heard his mother's pleading cry, of the
relationship of subjects to each other, to a whole.

The son has climbed the fence and strides now, quickly down the road. His back is turned; he will not see the farm again except in dream. The old man sees him go as he has seen it coming: the day hell would freeze over his dead body. There is an irony that withers there because the son has gone and cannot see the old man shaking off his wife, who hovers near to help him as he struggles to his feet and wipes a sleeve across his bloody mouth. Perspective requires a distance they do not possess, but we who watch them from the vantage point that words provide, can see each face and place them side by side. Both father and son refuse to register shame or the pain in bloody face or hand, though surely these are buried there. What is the countenance they share? It is not pain; the cast is far too sinister, as though some darker double stood behind the bones. Or the ghost of a twin drowned for its failings. These faces, old and young, are one— honed down to nearly nothing by willful subtraction. No, the look lodged there is not like shame, nor even pain, but something like pain's closest kin—I see it now—a kind of satisfaction.

What We Wish For

The boy could sometimes see, could sense
   his father's fondness for a thing.
      One Christmas he spurned comic books,
penciled "shotgun" on his list to prove
   he'd moved beyond the tin cans
      and the .22. En route to the rite of deer,
perhaps hunt birds…like tiny planes;
   safe in a blind, he'd take his time
      and zero in, and thus, he thought, he could
acquire the skill to bring a winged thing down.

What kind of birds he was not sure,
   nor could he have named his feelings
      as he crept downstairs at 5:00 a.m. to find
his gift unwrapped beneath the tree:
   a Winchester 12-gauge single shot,
      feather-light and purchased from a man
his father knew, a man with debts and mouths
   to feed, a man who'd said he needed cash.
      One man's desperation can become another's
gain, can lead a boy to standing
   with a shotgun and a box of shells,
      the desert his firing range, his pigeon
an old pie tin his father has tossed.

And as it spun into the late sun's glare,
   the boy took aim and saw it hover there
      in silhouette, like those photos in his sci-fi mags,
those saucers that he prayed were real.
   What he knew next was disbelief, as though
      he had recoiled from dream. His shoulder numb,
the hoax dawned in the dirt where he'd hit hard,
   his father looking dismally down,
      commanding him to rise and try again.

But when he forced himself to shoot
    a second time, teeth clenched and eyes closed,
        there was a click but no kick came.
By what volition he could not say, yet
    to the boy the silence seemed transgression
        of some natural law, of expectations overthrown—
for even in his father's hands the gun refused to fire.

They walked back to the truck at dusk,
    the boy somehow relieved, determined
        not to try again, his father, hurling curses
at the sky, then saying with resolve, as if
    a promise to himself, that he would get his
        money back, by God, he would.

Internment Camp Psychology

circa 1946

Just after his release Mas took a psychological test.

Three questions he never forgot: Do you think

people are out to get you? Do you feel you are

being followed? When you see a crowd of strangers

walking toward you, do you try to avoid them?

To all three he answered yes.

And knew he sounded insane.

The Left Panel of the Diptych Speaks

With my black pointed hood
and my raggedy black gown, its tatters
like the Wicked Witch might sport
before she hops on her broom
to write the sky in black smoke,
Surrender Dorothy!—I could be
holding out my hands for a trick
or treat, like any American
child on a Halloween eve,
if not for the wires that spring
from my palms to the wires
running up the tiled institutional wall
and the tall wooden box
where I perch as if on display
in some gallery in SoHo.
Just off to the side
you glimpse half the body
of a T-shirted guard or patron
inspecting his fingers—cutting
his nails?—as if bored
with the banality of modern art.
It's difficult to know what to make
of that, or how my photo
is paired with a pair of naked men
one kneeling to one with his head
in a square plastic sack,
face to crotch, though the one
below seems more bent in prayer,
despite the hands upon his head,
than into mouthing fellatio.
Perhaps all this is a commentary
on the institutional nature of sex
or the costumes some shed each day
to enact their dreams at night
or simply more evidence

of how the plague of homosexuality
is corrupting our highest
organs of culture. At any rate
nothing in the photo reveals
what I am breathing in
in this hood. Or how my keepers
have dutifully informed me
if I fall from this precarious spot
on my soapbox, I will be
instantly and justly jolted
by fifty thousand volts.

Sherman Ave. Love Poem #4

A cop car rounds
a corner, headlights
throw a man's silhouette
large against an apartment
building. A window opens
from his rib. A woman
steps through and pushes
off the ledge.

She floats four stories.
Doesn't flail. Doesn't
scream or scratch at passing
bricks. She is sure as gravity,
her fall as inevitable.

She floats. Four stories:
First hit. Starts to trick.
Limbs bloom lesions.
Now a belly swells
like a red rising sun.

Mid-flight, she lies flat,
spreads her shadow
across a fire hydrant.
The man crossing the street
clutches his Koran.
Does nothing to stop her.

He read in prison
how pregnant women
would dive from slave ships.
Thought then, and believes now
more than ever, that this is
the one true act.

JOAN MURRAY

Max and Rose

I didn't know then
how couples flow into the space around each other—
how Max's sweet exuberance
was only made possible by Rose's bitter chill.
Who knew what that whole generation
of refugees had gone through?
I knew nothing about them—
only that Max had been to Alaska,
had prospected for gold. Said words like
Klondike, Ketchikan, Kodiak. Stirred our imaginations
like the Yukon claim deed in our cereal box.
It was the South Bronx. I was seven. He called me
Joan of Arc. My brother, *Charles de Galle.*
For a dime, we'd get a Sunday scoop of ice cream,
and a chance for some tall tale. But Rose
with her long sighs roused only
one question: *Why* did he marry her?
If we'd see her heading to the counter,
we knew already all was lost. Silent as frost,
she'd slosh the metal scoop through the trough
of cloudy water, then dig, dig, dig—
like a prisoner hacking at a rock
that was ten-times-ten impossible—
and we were the ones who were forcing her.
If it were Max, the cone would sail forward
in his hand. Solid. Immense. Like the dense
block of an igloo. But Rose
with her sighs slipped in pockets
of air. Gaps. Evasions.
Places to hide.

Ode to the Eye

translated from the Spanish by Ilan Stavans

Powerful—
but a grain of sand,
a fly's foot,
half a milligram
of dust
entered your right eye
and the world
became dark and foggy.
Streets
became staircases,
buildings were covered with smoke,
your love, your son, your dinner plate
changed color,
turning
into palm trees or spiders.

Protect the eye!

The eye,
bubble of wonder,
small
octopus of our emptiness
extracting
brightness from shade,
polished
pearl,
alluring
blackness of the sea,
swift
engine
like nothing and no one,
dizzying

photographer,
French painter,
revelator of oracle.

Eye,
you name
the emerald glow,
trace
the growth
of an orange tree,
control
the laws of sunrise.
You measure,
announce danger,
encounter the glimmer
of others.
And fire burns in the heart,
like
an ancient mollusk.
You sneer
at the attacking acid.
You read,
read
the banker's numbers,
ABCs
by tender students from Turkey,
Paraguay, Malta.
Read
reports
and novels,
seize waves, rivers,
geographies.
Explorer,
you sight
your flag
in the remote sea, among the ships,
giving the shipwrecked sailor
the bluest portrait
of the sky.

Then, at night,
your small
closing
window
opens up from the other end, like a tunnel,
to the unsettled homeland of dreams.

I saw a dead man
in the salt
pampa,
a man made of salt,
a brother of sand.
During a strike,
while
I ate
with my compañeros,
he was struck down.
So they
soaked
their flags
in his blood,
coming back to the sand.
Across the arid pampa
they walked,
singing,
defying their oppressors.
I bent down
to touch his face.
In his dead
pupils,
I saw,
photographed
in their depth,
that his flag
was
still moving,
the same one
taken
by his brothers

into battle
while they sang.
There,
in the
well
that holds
humankind
forever,
I saw
his flag,
like scarlet fire,
an indestructible
poppy.

Eye,
you were missing
from his song.
When I returned to the ocean
I played my lyre's chords once again
and sang my ode.
You showed me,
delicately,
how foolish I am: I saw life, I saw the earth,
I saw
everything—
except my own eyes.
Then
you let a particle of dust
hide behind my eyelids.
I lost my sight.
The world grew
darker.
The eye doctor,
in his white uniform,
pointed his ray at me.
He allowed an infernal drop
to fall
down
like an oyster.

Later,
reflexive,
having recovered my sight—
and admiring
the brownish, spacious eyes
of my beloved—
I erased my ingratitude with this ode,
now being read,
mysteriously,
by you.

Ode to the Elephant

translated from the Spanish by Ilan Stavans

Thick, pristine beast,
Saint Elephant,
sacred animal
of perennial forests,
sheer strength,
fine
and balanced
leather
of global saddle-makers,
compact,
satin-finished ivory,
serene
like the moon's flesh,
with minuscule eyes
to see—and not be seen—
and a singing trunk,
a blowing horn,
hose of the creature
rejoicing in its own freshness,
shaking machine
and forest telephone,
this is how
the elephant passes by,
tranquil,
parading his ancient façade,
his costume
made of
wrinkled trees,
his pants
falling down,
and his teeny tail.

Make no mistake:
this gentle, huge jungle beast

is not a clown
but a father,
a priest of green light,
an earthly progenitor,
ancient
and whole.

Bountiful
in its tantalizing avarice,
made of skin and fornication,
the elephant kingdom
grew accustomed to the rain.
But then came
a universal war,
bringing
silence
with salt and blood.

The scaly forms
of lizard-lion,
mountain-fish,
magisterial Cyclops
fell away,
decayed,
fresh ferment on the marsh,
a treasure
for torrid flies
and cruel beetles.
The elephant awakened
from its dethroned fear,
but almost vegetative,
a dark tower
in the olive firmament, his lineage
nurtured by sweet leaves,
honey
and rock water.

Thus he wandered through the forest,
in weighty peace,

sensitive to the humidity of the universe,
decorated
with the clearest commands of the dew,
enormous, sad and tender,
until they found him
and turned him into a circus beast,
wrapped in human smells,
unable to breathe through his restless trunk,
without earth for his earthly feet.
I saw him coming in that day.
I remember his agony.

I saw the damned creature entering the Kraal,
in the jungle of Ceylon.
Drums and fire
had changed his path of dew,
and he was surrounded.
Like an immense king
he arrived,
caught between howl and silence.
He understood nothing.
His kingdom was a prison,
yet the sun was still the sun,
palpitating free light,
and the world was still verdant.
Slowly, the elephant touched the stockade
and chose me from everyone else.
I don't know why. Maybe it wasn't so,
could not have been,
but he looked at me
between the stakes
with his secret eyes.
His eyes
still pain me,
a prisoner's eyes,
the immense king captive in his own jungle.

That's why I invoke your gaze today,
elephant,

lost between the hard stakes
and the leaves.
In your honor, pristine beast,
I lift the collar
of my ode
so you may walk through the world again.
My unfaithful poetry
was unable to defend you then.
Now I bring you back
through memory,
along with the stockade caging
your animal honor,
measured only by your height,
and those gentle eyes,
deprived forever of all they had once loved.

Time on the Island

1
Tell me how the prison broke you.

The first night,
they played with a man
in the next cell.

Nine rollers scrunched
in the tiny stall, hardly room
to swing a fist—sometimes one
elbowed another and apologized—
the inmate wailed absentmindedly,
just a voice, and I listened.

I thought: I'd see you again.
I'd come back, we'd marry.

Before dawn everything was quiet.
My neighbor sobbed to himself
like a toddler who lost a toy,
softly, luxuriously (I thought),
with elaborate sniffs and hiccups.
I whispered through the bars
shh, then froze.

I thought, I'd always love you.

2

How were you set free?

At 4 a.m. they assembled us
on K-12. We lay face down
on the kitchen tables.
One clothed, the next naked.
A song played softly, a CO's tape.

Sometimes a name was called.

We were given our possessions
sterilized in a see-through bag
and a cardboard key—
to a vocational center,
or perhaps it was a joke?

My file was returned to me.
Just a dog-eared scrap
smudged from the Xerox;
your name and the date
of each visit.

Our child was entered
in that cramped blue script
with the precise unnecessary flounce.
I tore it to bits.

I came to myself
on the train to Brooklyn—
Marcy Avenue receding
in a rain of streaked lights.

I pictured you waiting for me.

3
It had become easy—
easy to suffer, to eat
that gray lunchmeat,
to say yes when a PT asked
for sex or a cigarette.

It seemed like falling
with no hope of hitting earth.

I tried to imagine
I was still a man in the world,
alone with the shocked face
of the stranger whose pocket
I slashed with my Spellman razor,
but I couldn't: just another story
I kept telling, to get your attention,
later we'd make love
and listen to the rain.

And I thought you would come home.

SHARON OLDS

The Couldn't

And then, one day, though my mother had sent me
upstairs to prepare, my thumbs were no longer
opposable, they would not hook into
the waistband, they swung, limp—under my
underpants was the Y of elastic, its
metal teeth gripping the pad,
I couldn't be punished unless I was bare, but I
couldn't be bare unless I took off my
Young Lady's First Sanitary Belt,
my cat's cradle, my goddess girdle,
and she couldn't want me to do that,
could she? But when she walked in, and saw me still
clothed, her face lit up with ironic
wonder, and combat. I did not speak,
she came toward me, I bolted, threw open her door,
slamming my brother to the floor with a keyhole
shiner, I poured down the staircase and through
some rooms, and got my back against
a wall, I would hurt her before the old scene
could play again. When she got there, maybe she could see that,
she had to look up, to look at me,
we faced off, dressed in our dresses and our
secret straps and pulleys of glory,
and then she stepped away from me—and for the
year that I stayed in that house, each month
our bodies called to each other, as if their
spirits brought each other bleeding off in the
waste of the power of creation.

The Alarm Clock

Two weeks after her husband's death,
just before I left for the airport,
my mother said, But how will I get
to the lawyer's on time tomorrow? I said Well you'll
leave the house in plenty of time, she
said No no, how will I wake up
in time? You'll set the alarm, Mom,
and she snapped at me, with annoyed contempt,
I don't know how to set an alarm, that was
his job. I looked at her. My
mother didn't know how to set an alarm clock.
I showed her. My hands tinkered behind
the aqua scrollwork, the heaven-fray,
she watched with a child's attention. At the airport
I bought her a small travel alarm,
easy as pie, pallid and round
as a raw tartlet, and sent it to her.
Years later, she confides in me
that when it arrived, she kissed its little face,
and every night, when she goes to bed,
she kisses its face.

ISHLE YI PARK

Stars

When my mother turned sixty, she kissed the invisible stars
on the foreheads of her two grown men and deemed them
   worthy stars

The sky, a vaulted blue dome, empties
itself and fills Pyongyang with quick, fluid stars

Tonight, longing fans out like a silk curtain
over an empty room; a girl's eyes burn like hungry stars

In Gum Gang San restaurant, Mr. Park croons—
If I could reach into night with my two hands and harvest
   all the stars…

When parents age like wine, they tuck away
desires and settle for accountant-sons (lesser stars)

Scales on a black sea bass
in a dim-lit freezer *winkwink* like frozen stars

Lying on a rice mat in South Korea
we witness the descent of three, long-tailed stars

Years ago, she put her breast in my mouth
and fed me stars; soon she will spill into a larger milk of stars

A red flag once burned a hole in my mother's youth—
its ashes now hold: a gold sickle, a hammer, a star

2 *Korean Girls*

June. A white heat.
Two schoolgirls with crisp collars
tread home on a red road.

> Two young boys with crewcuts
> yawn in the third tank, blink
> from five hours sleep.

Blue dragonflies, girlsweat,
orange dust on Adidases...

> Green interior. Boysweat.
> A twist of knobs and dials.

Down the road,
a shack holds *miyuk guk*
for a classmate's birthday...

> After this last run, they'll play spades,
> stare out at the green nothing.

They laugh, skirt the road's lip,
arms out like tiny drunks.

> A Bradley throws signs, shouts
> three times into headphones

Uphill,
switchgrass
stings bare calves,

> (the boys forgot
> to check mikes
> before load-out)

girls scramble,
but the tank

> swallows all road

shoelaces   a blue skirt hem

dragonflies

flies

a green field
shush   shush   shush

black hair fans
like a torn fish fin

June 13th, 2002:
2 Korean girls
run over on the smaller
road to Mansu-ri.
at the girl's party,
mi sun & ho soon's warm rice
bowls cool. harden.
Army officials
answer press: *No comment. No*
comment. No comment.
mi sun's *umma* hurls her body
over her daughter's crushed body
No one pleads guilty.
No one convicted.

midnight in seoul
50,000 gold candles
ring the embassy
(One soldier can't sleep—
types online grief-notes to families)
one placard reads:
for 50 years, you claim the throne.
yankeee, please—go home.
Two boys fly back home.
Play spades, stare into nothing.
Tell their girls nothing.

tank treads   crushed stems
an abandoned red road
june   a white heat

A Vision of Horses and Mules

Learn to think like a horse
her trainer said. She went
into the pasture at noon,
when her horses lay down to sleep
without fear of coyotes,
without fear. They sensed her
but did not mind as she stretched
out beside them with the June
heat's broad strong hand
flattening her into the grass.

Now, she said, I am studying
mules. Her trainer told her
horses forget everything by
and by. Mules never forget.
Carry your intention carefully,
a brimming bowl of water.
Muleskinner, I called her
and from my childhood I saw
a tin of Boraxo my father used
to clean grease from his hands.

Twenty-mule teams crossed
the Death Valley of our bathroom, little black mules along
the bottom of the tin, the driver
in his wagon, the whip cracking
a wicked S in the air. I'm a mule:
stubborn, dragging heavy grudges,
joys and lost friends from the alkaline
mines of my past across the bleak
present to some future vital use.

The Avalanche

He braked the old green Chevy
   on the side of a mountain
      somewhere out West

and bet my mother he could
   start a serious avalanche
      by kicking a single rock into another

no she said no please don't Dan
   please don't start an avalanche
      please and in the back seat I

an only child trapped
   with a pile of Archie and Veronicas
      watched my mother's chin crumple

while out the window my father hunted
   the sun-crazed slope for that one rock
      that would knock our whole world loose

Fuses

The last spike hammered into the last day
meant not one more Chinese laborer would be
lowered in a basket down the side of a mountain
to separate the mountain from itself with
a brand of dynamite that knew its own mind, never
hesitating to render asunder whatever the Whiteman's
God had assembled on that famous day of the first
week that anything happened anywhere and everywhere.

And with fuses that never learned they didn't have
to burn up the last years of their lives in two heartbeats,
probably less, burning without reason, with no remorse,
shamelessly allowing themselves the pleasure
of digging their fingernails into somebody else's heart,
burning with wicked madness, faster than a man
can claw his way back up the mountain, than he can be
pulled hand over hand with a rope made out of
the ashes of the wind, faster than a newly canonized
saint ascending into the heathen's heaven. Fuses that
burn fast because they burn fast, they know no other way
of introducing themselves, of saying farewell. Farewell
is never as easy as hello. They want to shake a man's
hand, not only out of politeness, but out of a perverted sense
of genealogy, I am you, you are me, and we are One.
They want to shake a man's hand, offering peace. I am you,
you are me, we are One but by the time they extend
their hand, the basket, and the man who oftentimes in his
dreams saw himself flying home, are already scattered
from Gold Mountain to everywhere and anywhere.

ADRIENNE RICH

Life of the Senses

1.

Over and over, I think
we have come to a place
                like this,
dead sound

stopping the soul
in its eager conversations

Or, a classical theme
repeated over and over   interrupted
by a voice disguised as human:
                      Please
stay on the line
Your call is very
important to us

2.

Don't know if I can describe it, this
that in my busyness and ordinary

life of the senses
impales me
a riff of loneliness or loss

in a body older yet sensuous still
But you know it, young swimmer, and you, bass-player

you carefully weighing out your ounce of mushrooms
and you who harvest them in the damp cellars

you in your headset answering
800 numbers from prison

you who monitor recorded calls
for quality assurance

you, skateboarding in darkness
and you, taking blood pressures in the free clinic

and you, gliding on escalators
under the glazed roof of the humanist hotel

you, who have everything yet will die
frightened and empty-handed and you

who would give anything you hold in your hands
to belong to a world
that isn't yet

and not because we haven't heard
that kind of music

3.

No, it's worse than I'm saying:
Have you ever woken on a hot night

tangled in a sheet you'd been trying
to throw off

wanting to clutch the dream
you'd been wrapped in

as long as possible?

4.

Sometimes merely
ordinary
words must serve

in sickness   health
and the gray between

> *where does it hurt*
> *have you eaten*
>
> *you're a mess*
> *travel safe, O.K.?*
>
> *I'll try and fix it*
> *could you give me some dough*
>
> *I'm thirsty*
> *wake up we're having a nightmare*

The small hours
can be long

dawn actually gray the way
they say

Mozart and the Mockingbird

This morning, I turned down Mozart to listen
              to a mockingbird perched on a wire
outside my window. Poor Mozart. Dead,
      he was much the worse for comparison.
But as soon as I lowered the music,
              the mockingbird flew.
He had been listening to Mozart.

R. T. SMITH

Dar He

When I am the lone listener to the antiphony of crickets
and the two wild tribes of cicadas and let my mind
wander to its bogs, its sloughs where no endorphins fire,

I will think on occasion how all memory is longing
for the lost energies of innocence, and then one night—
whiskey and the Pleiades, itch from a wasp sting—

I realize it is nearly half a century since that nightmare
in Money, Mississippi, when Emmett Till was dragged
from his uncle Mose Wright's cabin by two strangers

because he might have wolf whistled at Carolyn Bryant,
a white woman from whom he had bought candy,
or maybe he just whispered "Bye," as the testimony

was confused and jangled by fear. The boy was not local,
and Chicago had taught him minor mischief, but what
he said hardly matters, and he never got to testify,

for the trial was for murder after his remains were dredged
from the Tallahatchie River, his smashed body with one
eye gouged out and a bullet in the brain and lashed

with barbed wire to a cotton gin fan whose vanes
might have seemed petals of some metal flower, had Bobo
—as friends at home called him—ever seen it. And why

this might matter to me tonight is that I was not yet eight
when the news hit and can remember my parents at dinner—
maybe glazed ham, probably hand-whipped potatoes,

iced tea sweeter than candy, as it was high summer—
shaking their heads in passing and saying it was a shame,
but the boy should have been smarter and known never

to step out of his place, especially that far South. Did I
even guess, did I ask how a word or stray note could give birth
to murder? He was fourteen, and on our flickering new TV,

sober anchormen from Atlanta registered their shock,
while we ate our fine dinner and listened to details
from the trial in Sumner, though later everyone learned

the crime occurred in Sunflower County, and snoopy
reporters from up north had also discovered that missing
witnesses—Too Tight Collins among them—could

finger the husband Roy Bryant and his stepbrother
named Milam as the men in the truck who asked, "Where
the boy done the talking?" and dragged Emmett Till

into the darkness. His mother, Mamie, without whom
it would have all passed in the usual secrecy, requested
an open-casket funeral, so the mourners all saw the body

maimed beyond recognition—his uncle had known
the boy only by a signet ring—and *Jet* magazine
then showed photos, working up the general rage

and indignation, so the trial was speedy, five days
with a white jury, which acquitted, the foreman
reporting that the state had not adequately established

the identity of the victim, and I don't know how
my father the Cop or his petite wife the Den Mother
took it all, though in their eighties they have no love

for any race darker than a tanned Caucasian. I need
a revelation to lift me from the misery of remembering,
as I get the stigma of such personal history twisted

into the itch of that wasp sting. Milam later told *Life*
he and Bryant were "guilty as sin," and there is some
relief in knowing their town shunned them and drove

Bryant out of business, but what keeps haunting me—
glass empty, the insect chorus fiercer, more shrill—
is the drama played out in my mind like a scene

from some reverse *To Kill a Mockingbird*—or worse,
a courtroom fiasco from a Faulkner novel—when
the prosecutor asked Mr. Wright if he could find

in the room the intruder who snatched his nephew
out of bed that night, and the old man—a great uncle,
really—fought back his sobs and pointed at the accused,

his finger like a pistol aimed for the heart. "Dar he,"
he said, and the syllables yet echo into this raw night
like a poem that won't be silenced, like the choir

of seven-year insects, their voices riddling strange
as sleigh bells through the summer air, the horrors
of injustice still simmering, and I now wonder what

that innocence I miss might have been made of—
smoke? rhinestones? gravied potatoes followed
by yellow cake and milk? Back then we called

the insect infestation *ferros,* thinking of Hebrew
captivity in Egypt and believing they were chanting
free us, instead of the *come hither* new science

insists on, but who can dismiss the thought
that forty-nine years back their ancestors dinned
a river of sound all night extending lament

to lamentation, and I am shaken by the thought
of how easy it is for me to sit here under sharp
stars which could mark in heaven the graves

of tortured boys and inhale the dregs of expensive
whiskey the color of a fox, how convenient
to admit where no light shows my safe face

that I have been less than innocent this entire
life and never gave a second thought to this:
even the window fan cooling my bedroom

stirs the air with *blades,* and how could anyone
in a civilized nation ever be condemned for
narrowing breath to melody between the teeth,

and if this is an exercise in sham shame I am
feeling, some wish for absolution, then I have to
understand the wave of nausea crossing me,

this conviction that it is not simple irony
making the whir of voices from the pine trees
now seem to be saying *Dar he, Dar he, Dar he.*

GARY SOTO

Some Words About Time

Bored, I open the back of an ancient clock
And the minutes pile out,
Exhausted from spinning
Out the same hammered seconds.
The minutes stagger on the table
And collapse, for they are dizzy,
For they have realized they have no legs,
For the surface of the table is flat
And what have they known but a round world.
I touch one of the minutes—an ant
With feeling antenna—and with my hand
Bulldoze them all to the kitchen floor.

Again, I am bored. I examine the oily guts
Of the clock, tinker with the sprockets
And springs, and revel in the master plan
To keep lackeys punching the clock.
I think of myself at the car wash
Bringing a soapy sponge to
The toothy grill of an old Pontiac.
I used four seconds on each of the dirty teeth,
And ten seconds on each droopy headlight.
This was how I viewed time
At age seventeen, the boy in morning
Sunlight and, two minutes to eight,
Reaching for a sponge,
Sponge that was a wheezing lung—
Even before the clock started
My hand struggled with an exhausted tool.

Old Dog Sniffing the Air

It was in that year the dog arrived
On the farm, and I appeared in his eyes,
A speck because I was made of flesh,
Not fur, not tail, not paws thick as leather.
I bent down, patted his coat,
And I asked, Is it time now?
The old stray was reddish brown,
His breathing shallow,
And his tail a short whip
Against my pants leg.
Is it time now? I repeated,
Thinking of that journey
Down the tractor path,
He to the left of me
Taking six steps for every one of mine.
But first, he licked the drops
From a leaky faucet,
And I tied my shoes,
These twin boats scuffed
From my anger at kicking the world.
When I called him once,
He followed me to the end
Of the vineyard,
The grapes puny on the vines.
If I stuck my hand
In among the sulfured leaves,
Spiders would pull in their legs
And rabbits leap away.
I tossed a clod among the vines
And watched a blackbird lift,
The undertaker's favorite bird.
I walked to the end of the first row
And the dog, my future, followed
With his tags clinking under his chin.
It was sunset, or nearly sunset,

And my shirt ruffled in the valley wind
That shuffles our shoeprints—
Every day we stamped our place
In this sandy soil,
And wind wiped our tracks clean.
I looked back. I saw a house
Among vineyards, my wife pinning wash.
I had done much, done little,
And my shirts on the line
Had more wind in them than I did.
I crumbled a clod. I sniffed the air,
And the dog sniffed,
Nose pointed skyward.
What were we smelling on a fall day
But our years dying on the mortgaged vines?

GERALD STERN

The Law

The world is always burning, you should fly
from the burning if you can, and you should hold
your head oh either above or below the dust
and you should be careful in the blocks of Bowery
below or above the Broome that always is changing
from one kind of drunkenness to another
for that is the law of suffering, and you know it.

Blackout

New York City, August 13, 2003

All this
is not unusual in DR or Iraq.
The city's extension cord shorts.
Afternoon, offices evacuate.
The focus is on feet,
some people walking through boroughs
for the first time. We stare at our feet,
elbow to elbow eyeing packed buses.
Some hitch rides on the back
of trucks. An orderly mob of feet,
legs pushing past fearless
grocery stores. Lincoln
Center, Harlem, finally

in Washington Heights the street
party has begun. Batteries boost
the curbside music, click of candlelit
dominoes, night meeting a stream
of car lights, congestion
of bodies. Everyone is polite and briefly
romantic in the dark. On my block,
there's a woman selling hot pasteles
on paper plates, with ketchup
if you want.

A Spell to Wake My Brother

We will weave through
the labyrinth of headstones
to clear the patch of soil
where you rest,
to plant a tall palm
with leaves that know
that north sea breeze,
to roast a suckling pig.

The blood of this pig
will mingle with your bones,
tickle your limbs, awake
the bomba y plena pulse.
We will bring the ocean to you,
hermano who lies far
from your birthright home.
Listen, Miguelito
to the sea stirring.

Forget this Brooklyn.
Let's eat cuero,
the crisp skin, and drink.
When our last brother's hands
strike the drum,
wake to the beat
of your favorite bolero.

LEWIS TURCO

Brontophobia: The Fear of Thunder

The first time she could remember hearing thunder
she'd been sitting on her grandma's lap
in the formal parlor of the big old house where she
was visiting. She flinched and shuddered. "What's that,
Grandma?" she'd asked. "That is the voice of God,"

the old woman said, and then they heard it again
rolling out of the clouds, across the sky
and into the formal parlor hung with drapes
where the portrait of her dead grandfather hung above
the mantel and stared at her

as though with the eyes of God. She blanched and shuddered,
and had been shuddering ever since, whenever
the great dark clouds rolled over the deep blue sky,
shutting all the earth into a parlor
hung with mists and rain, where a dead old man

stared down at them out of the roaring heavens
and told them what he thought without a word,
with only the sound of warning, the sound of dread,
the clap resounding out of admonition
and into the parlor in which they were entombed.

CHASE TWICHELL

New England Slate Pane

Mom has already made arrangements
for a spot inside the churchyard wall
among the old Yankee slates,
some fallen, and the granites
from foreign places,
tilted by frost.
A mason sets them straight
again each spring.
Perennials for the formal beds
accepted with gratitude;
no other plantings allowed.
Cut flowers may be laid on the graves.
Someone might leave
plastic tulips as a joke.
Otherwise, silence, nothing,
trees living their interior lives,
visitors wandering
among the oldest stones.
This is where she wants to lie,
next to wind-pruned beach roses,
paths of crushed shells.

Somebody finally bought that farm
and orchard I like to drive past
at blossom time,
mud runnels in the roads,
trees way past mature.
For ten years no one's come
to prune or feed or mow the aisles.
Bare scatterings of flowers
alight on broken branches.
Who let it all go?
What broke in the family?

Now the elderly apples will spend
their twilight in the paintings of a man
who bought them
in order to study their end.
She wants her marker spare like that,
just name and dates.
Time's black and white bouquet.

DAVID WILLIAMS

Some Writers in Wartime

What is essential as breath reduced
to a squabble about moral parity

to hold a brief for the party
that orders death. Moral parody:

ours is but to cook, serve, clear,
speak when spoken to.

*

We will not swell the glory chorus,
slaughter calling to slaughter
like lovers possessed.

Nor will we turn away.
At least there will be a record
if the children ask someday.

*

Survive by paradox. Give the lie
to righteous might. Heart muscle cells,
one to the next, transmit

a spark to roll waves—systolic,
diastolic, moonlit, sunlit—
in the body's dark, oceanic.
                              Pass it on.

ALYSON HAGY

Border

It was not as hard to steal the collie pup as he thought it would be. From early morning when the woman set up and wiped her table with a cloth until the time the silver container of coffee was emptied by those coming to look at the dogs, there had been somebody around the camper and around the crate that held the pups. But lunch hour put the scatter in people. Tacos and fry bread were for sale on the other side of the bleachers—he could smell them. And the heat slowed things down, even for the dogs that panted hard and fast like they knew they were destined for the sheep-herding finals.

The high sun was what seemed to drive the woman into the camper. It was nothing more than company, the chance to talk out of the hearing of adults, that got rid of the girl and her sister. They went off with kids they seemed to know from the sheep-raising universe of Colorado. There was discussion of buying Cokes or lemonades. The older girl was the one who'd offered him a pup to hold. He'd refused, staying polite and not looking too interested. He had a dog at home, he said, one that was good over pheasant and jumping in the water for ducks. A hunting dog from Texas. This was a lie from his mouth, though he'd heard the exact same words said by a long-haul friend of his father's.

Except for the dog stories, he had not liked that friend.

The girl had smooth brown hair held off her neck in braids the way 4-H girls he knew wore their hair, especially the ones who barrel-raced on horses. He was a little sorry she would get in trouble because of him. She'd take the blame, no matter what. That was how it worked. But there was a pile of pups in that crate. At $400 apiece, nobody's feelings or whipped ass was going to hurt for long.

Luck would determine if it was male or female. He wouldn't have time to check. A bitch was easier to train. This, too, came from his father's friend. But there was some number of male dogs in the finals. He'd watched them stalk the skittery bands of sheep

148

in the preliminaries. He knew how capable they were. And he didn't care what it was. The one the girl held away from her chest to show him had looked good enough to him. Everybody knew border collies were smart beyond the ordinary for dogs. You could train them to within an inch of their business, and they would wait outside a building for you with no rope or leash. They would wait for you all day.

He partly zipped his jacket and snapped the snap on its waist-band. His Broncos hat was already so low on his head he could barely see. He slipped in and unpinned the crate before he even squatted down. The lucky one was towards the front, round-bellied, asleep on its side. He used two hands for support so as not to shock the pup, wanting it to think well of him from the get-go. He lifted it like it was a glass tray. Then he got one hand under its sleepy, dangled haunches and slid it into his jacket. It didn't make a peep, nor did its many sisters and brothers. He closed the crate, put a quick touch on the bill of his Broncos hat to be sure it was set square on his head, and he was gone.

He waited until he was clear of the Meeker fairgrounds to take off his zippered jacket and turn it inside out so that the brown cloth fabric showed instead of the blue. He also removed his hat and tucked it in his back pocket, though his bare head felt show-offy to him. This was his disguise. He had to set the pup on the ground to make his changes. It was more alert now, and he saw its tongue bend in an arch when it yawned, and he saw its tiny teeth. The teeth were see-through and small like fish teeth. He scooped the pup with his hands and cradled it. It was a female. He could tell that much. He could also tell from the mask of her face that she had the good, preferred markings he'd heard the handlers talk about.

She made a sound in her white-furred throat, and he made a sound back.

He carried her through town inside his brown jacket, cars and trucks passing on both sides of the road. He supported her round belly with his hands, walking as if his hands were only in his jack-et pockets and he was only going for a stroll. He used sidewalks when he could. He wished he could stop at the café he saw—one with yellow-painted windowpanes around the windows—but he knew he could not, even though he had money, because of the deputies and what had happened with his father. He read the sign for the café that hung out over the street, and he liked the sound of the name. Belle's. He could call the pup that, call her Bell after the instrument and after the café in the town where he'd gotten her. Border collies always came with short names. It cut down on confusion.

Bell. A good name for a dog that was bound to be sweet but never shy.

He walked until he got to the gas stations. There was one on each side of the road just before the road filled out into a highway. He saw what he hoped to see on a good-weather Sunday, a steady stream of livestock trailers and open-backed trucks, many of them too large and awkward to pull next to the pumps. He'd planned to take time to buy food, but he knew better than to pass on what looked like a rare chance. A red trailer stacked with hay was goose-necked to a diesel pickup with Colorado plates. The driver had left the rig angled near the air hose. He did what he'd done before, apologizing to Bell in a low voice for the delay of their supper. He unlatched the trailer's gate on one side and stepped into the dark crowdedness of the hay. Then he slid Bell loose from under his jacket and set her safe in the trailer's corner. He turned, made a loop of the orange rope that was already tied to the rear of the trailer, caught the latch handle in that loop, snugged the gate closed, and dropped the latch to lock them inside. It would be a hell of a sight easier to travel with hay than with steers or horses. They might not even get caught.

He sat down and drew Bell onto his lap, leaning into the sweet wall of hay. Bell had slept in the nest of his jacket, but she was awake now. Her dazedness was wearing off. He could feel the difference in the set of her legs and the sharp probing of her teeth on the soft parts of his hands. She would miss her brothers and sisters soon. He knew how that would go. Missing a sister—he did not have a brother—was a burn that was slow to cool. What he needed most was for Bell not to bark. Barking would not be good, not until they were out of town. He tried to keep her busy chewing on the bottoms of his jeans and on his hands, though her sharp fish teeth were already making him sore. He was glad when the driver cranked the rig and they eased onto the highway. The weather was dialed in. There would be no problems with heat or cold. They could find food later, though he understood food was something he knew how to do without while Bell did not. But if he was right, the trailer's destination was close—no more than a couple of hours. He pulled his Broncos hat from his pocket and smoothed it down over his hair. He knew how to wait.

When the rig slowed to leave the highway, he took a look and thought the town might be Hayden. The driver pulled into another gas station but didn't cut the engine—it seemed like the driver only needed to take a leak. He bundled up Bell and got out of the trailer while the going was good. The sun was still flat and clear in the sky, but the air was beginning to smell of evening. He walked behind the station and took a leak of his own, then he let Bell walk and sniff some in the gravel. He needed to get one of those whistles, the kind only a dog could hear. For now, he'd count on his voice and the way Bell would learn to listen to it.

"Come on, Bell. Come on, little gal." He knelt on the gravel and called until she came to him. He told her she was pretty smart to make him proud on her first day.

He apologized for what he had to do next. He set her in an empty barrel that was soured from garbage, and he walked fast around the station and went inside and bought a pint of milk and some sticks of peppered jerky and two bottles of the fancy water his father made fun of. He paid for his selections with the bills folded in his front pants pocket. He was tight with worry for Bell, he didn't like to leave her. He got back, and he stroked her on top while she drank water from a hamburger container until they both were calm. There was hay mixed in her black fur and a flat mark of grease on her tail. He tried to clean her with his fingers. He had some water, too, while Bell lapped at milk, then he got after the jerky. Bell didn't care for the jerky. He told himself that next time he would get the kind without pepper.

He had passed through Hayden before, and he liked his chances of finding a ride. He knew people paid no attention to strangers and how they came and went, alone or not alone, in the summer. He only wondered how bold he should be. His question was answered by the arrival of a club-cab Ford bearing two cowboys. He was standing near the phone booth when it pulled in.

He watched the driver for a short time. The driver was a rodeo cowboy, for sure. Ironed shirts hung in the window of the Ford, and there was a show hat on the driver's head. The passenger was dressed cowboy, too, though that meant nothing except a passenger was cause to travel faster. He walked up to the driver and asked for a ride.

"It's just me and this little dog," he said.

The driver, who was young and red-skinned from the day's sun, looked him over. "Where to?"

"I got cousins on the Front Range, cousins and a aunt. Any place toward Denver is good. The dog is for them."

"Denver it is," said the driver.

"Tell him he's got to buy beer." This came from the passenger.

"I don't believe he's old enough to buy beer."

"Shit. You know what I mean."

"I got money," he said. And he dug into his pocket with some defiance. He freed up ten dollars, handed it to the young driver.

"Cute dog."

"She is," he said. "Smart, too."

"What if she messes in the truck?" This from the passenger again, in a mood.

"I'll hold her. If she wets, she'll wet on me."

"I got a towel," the driver said. "I don't know what Ray's worried about. A little dog like that can't out-mess him no how."

"Fuck you," said the passenger, making one piece of a smile. "And give over that money. I've got a thirst."

They got going pretty fast, him and Bell squeezed in the back of the cab with some rigging and a bull rider's vest. He held Bell so she could look out the window as they drove, and she seemed to like that. The driver and Ray cracked beers and drank them and didn't talk. They started to talk when they slowed to pass through Steamboat Springs because they wanted to make fun of the town for its traffic lights and tourists. The driver said he didn't know a single good horseman who could still afford to live in Steamboat.

"They got girls, though," said Ray. He was watching out the windows just like Bell.

"Not the kind you like," said the driver.

"What's that mean?"

"It means rich. It means talking and spoiling and taking your time."

"And I can't do that?"

"Besides your being butt-ugly, I've never seen you slow down for nothing, even a rich girl."

"Fuck you."

"It's true," the driver said, laughing. "We have plowed this field before—"

"I ain't plowed nothing with you. You can't—"

"My point is you could act right, but you don't."

"And who are you? Mister Smooth Shit?"

"I didn't say one way or the other."

Ray looked over his shoulder. "You say you're giving up that dog. I wouldn't give up a good dog or a good gun, neither one. With those situations you know what's next. They stay in bed all damn night whether you want them or not."

"You got to excuse Ray," the driver said, laughing some more. "He just got throwed off the crippledest mare on the West Slope."

"Didn't do so hot yourself, twig dick."

"I didn't. It's lucky I got a credit card for gas."

They went into their third beers as the truck hauled up Rabbit Ears Pass. He stashed their empties at his feet. Bell whined some at the change in altitude until Ray asked if he could hold her. He didn't want to give her up, but he knew travel meant all range of favors. So he gave Ray the pup, and she seemed to take to him, working at his skin and his sleeves with her tongue and teeth. Ray gave him a cold beer in return, and he drank it, grateful.

He would guess later that it was the losing Ray couldn't get past because he couldn't find anything else about the situation that might have flipped the switch. Ray hadn't had that much beer, none of them had. It was just that he had to make somebody else the loser.

"This is a nice dog," Ray said after Bell curled into his lap for some sleep. "How old?"

"Seven weeks," he said. "She still misses her mama."

"I don't miss mine. How much she cost you?"

He paused, listening for the trap. Older boys and men liked to set traps. "Four hundred," he said.

Ray made a whistle sound behind his lips. It was not the admiring kind. The sound perked Bell up. "How much did those heelers go for in Rifle? I saw Bobby Byrd take one, but I don't recall the price."

The driver turned his head for one second. "I don't remember, had to be a couple hundred. You know, when you wake a pup—"

"Oh, damn. Shit."

"That ain't shit."

"Damn. Make her stop. Come on, dog, stop."

"Naw," the driver said, choking. "Your britches ain't wet with shit."

Ray cussed a long streak, holding Bell in the air like a paper airplane while he tried to work the piss off his legs. The towel, they'd all forgotten that. The driver, still aiming fast into the valley, reached under his seat and found an oil rag, which he tossed at Ray. "Oh," said the driver. "Oh, I got one now. Pissed pants and a crippled mare. I got one to tell on you now."

"Goddamn dog," Ray said. "Right on my best jeans."

"I'll take her," he said from the back seat. "She didn't mean to hurt nothing."

"The hell she didn't. She's one bad thing after another on a bad day. So are you. Dillon there made you part of my damn bad day."

"Then let us off," he said, his heart bolting the way it did when he was close to trouble. "That's what you can do."

"That's not what I *want* to do," yelled Ray.

"Christ, Ray, it's no more than pup piss. It'll dry."

"It is more. It's what you said."

"Christ, then. I take it back. I didn't mean to get under your saddle."

"Yeah, you did, you son of a bitch. In the money at Gunnison two weeks ago and you ain't let up since. You don't think I'm good enough to haul with your gear."

"Give the kid his dog."

"No."

"Give it to him."

"I'll give him something else first," Ray said, his hand going after his belt buckle, and that meant two things to him in the back seat—it meant belt whipping or worse—and he'd given up taking the hurt of both, so he reared between the seats and grabbed for little Bell. But Ray was quicker, and mean. He kept his hands free, and he got his window down, and he dropped the dog out onto the moving road.

"Christ. Jesus Christ, Ray. You can't do that," yelled the driver. But he had.

The driver, Dillon, hit the brakes, which sent them all flying forward, and cut down on the punches and kicks that followed. They threw him out of the truck, too. Ray kept yelling, his face the color of meat, but he heard nothing of it. He ran. He was all running. He saw her by the side of the road, black and white like a shoe tossed into the bristly cheatgrass. He saw her move. Then he was by her and with her, lying on the ground low and flat so she might see his face. Pleading. "Don't be dead, Bell. Please don't be dead."

She staggered to her feet. She shook her head as though her ears itched, then bounded deeper into the bristled grass. She went away from him and away from the road. Scared.

"She rolled. Swear to God she rolled, I saw it in my mirror. She might be all right." It was the driver, Dillon. He had backed his truck up to where they were. Ray wasn't with him. "Young ones like that don't have much bone. She might not've felt it."

He lifted her up, afraid to see blood in her mouth, afraid she'd have eyes like his sister's cats after they had been drop-kicked.

"I'd take you to a vet, but I can't, not with Ray. I'm sorry. The town's right up here. Walden. I'm sorry. Here's money to have her looked at."

There were sounds. The truck disappeared. He made out that it stopped for Ray before it started again, and he made out the pale leaf of a twenty-dollar bill on the darkness of the road. He picked up the bill and put it in a separate pocket. Bell's heart was like a hammer against his hands, and his own heart was moving blood so fast it made his stomach sick. He was afraid the live part of Bell would tear through the skin of her chest and leave him behind, but it didn't.

After a minute or two she acted like she wanted to walk. He didn't let her down at first, but then he did. She walked like normal. She sniffed at the oily road. When she saw a grasshopper and tried to stalk it, he knew she was all right. Bent, but not broke. He told her he was glad. That he was proud of how tough she was and how she learned things. What she'd learned was a lesson he hadn't meant to teach her right away even though it was bound to come before you were ready for it, the black lesson of fear.

He let her play until his face was dry.

There were lights in some of the Walden houses, and the air was as cool as the river. The streets were quiet. He and Bell weren't likely to catch a ride now. He walked along the main street where the businesses were closed until he saw a pizza place. It was open, and there were kids inside, regular kids, paying $7.95 for the special advertised in the window. He wished he could spend his money that way. Maybe when they got to Denver he would. As a treat for himself even more than Bell.

He walked past the pizza place with Bell snug in his jacket. He turned left, smelling hot bread, then turned left again at the alley. The dumpster was near the kitchen, where he could hear people talking and banging things as they worked. After dark, he would check the dumpster. Leftover pizza wasn't bad if you got it out of the box quick.

If a deputy or anybody asked, he was waiting for his father, who was fishing. There was a lot of fishing around Walden. He knew that even though he was from across the state line in Wyoming and had only been fishing with his father one time that he remembered.

His mother had never been part of anything.

He started walking again to avoid deputies and the kids moving through the spreading dark on their bikes. This was how he found the funny house. To him it looked no bigger than a square with windows, and it was painted orange with trim that had some purple parts and some red. It was the kind of place that made people shake their heads. There was a white fence, too, no higher than his knees, and a small sign on the fence written in swirly letters. He put Bell down along the fence while he tried to read the letters. This was when she started to talk.

"Is that you, Donny? Donald Bunch? Is that you raising money for the band?"

The woman was at the purple door of the house. She was holding on to the doorframe with both hands.

"No, ma'am. It's not who you think."

"Are you coming in? We're still open."

"I don't know. I just got here. I have my dog."

"You should come in," she said, turning. "I'm not busy. I like dogs."

He got Bell from the ground, and he opened the gate in the low fence and went in. He wanted to be polite. The woman stopped him at the screen part of her door and said again how much he looked like Donny Bunch or any of the Bunch brothers.

"Do you know him from school? He lives on Spur Ranch. Likes to ask me for money."

"No, ma'am, I don't know him. I'm not from here."

"Just as well," she said. "New faces mean new facts. Come in so I can see you."

He thought then that there was something wrong with her eyes and the way they seemed not to look right at him. He wondered if she was blind or partly blind. He was still wondering when he went into the house that smelled like a flower shop that kept both old flowers and new ones. The front room was crowded at the edges. There were square tables of different heights. There were books and piled magazines.

"Do you have a name?"

"I do. Tyler. Tyler . . . Bell."

"And your dog?"

He realized his mistake and corrected for it. "She don't have her right name yet, I just got her."

"We might have to give her one, then. She's very pretty," the woman said, touching Bell between the ears like she knew what she was doing. Like she wasn't all blind. "Will you have something to drink? We're open."

He could tell there was no other person in the house to make up a "we." He wasn't sure what it would cost to drink something. He didn't see any lists. But he would pay if he had to. Ever since smelling that pizza, he'd wanted to spend money.

"I can't stay long," he said. "But a soda is okay if you have some."

"Would tea be all right . . . and water for your friend? I have that. I'm sorry to hear you're in a hurry. You didn't look it."

He started to tell the story about waiting for his father, but something made him stop. He said nothing rather than saying a lie. His father hated places like the funny house. He would hate the woman and say terrible, rude things to her. But now...now he was a great distance from his father. He had changed how the two of them were. Thinking of that made his hands go thick and hot.

The woman came back with water in a dish for Bell. Her return stirred up the smells again, the papery thin ones he didn't know. Bell was all over the floor of the house, playing, but it seemed to be working out. The woman said tea would be ready soon—he could have any kind he liked—and she apologized for the noise of a radio he could barely hear.

"It's the war," she said. "Sometimes I can't stop listening to it."

He looked at her and her funny eyes when she said that. There was something in them, or not in them. "Do you have somebody over there?" he asked.

"No, Tyler, I don't. But thank you for asking. My boy fights what he fights down in Pueblo. I don't see him much." She made one hand into the shape of a cup. "I listen because I think I can learn what a damn thing is about. They've got me fooled. I still think that. Maybe you'll tell me I'm wrong."

"No, ma'am," he said. "I wouldn't do that."

"You're shy," she said. "But I can tell that doesn't keep you from taking care of yourself."

"The pup," he said. "I'm taking care of her."

"Yes. I see that. You're very good with the dog."

Then there was tea—he picked a mint one—and milk to put in it and lemony cookies and peanuts in a clay bowl. He ate more than he should have. He let her see he was hungry, but he planned to pay her so there would not be an obligation. He liked how she did everything calm and slow, though after a while it was hard for him to keep from yawning.

While he drank tea, the woman lit a match and put it to a straw she took from a bunch of straws. She stuck the straw in the pot of a green plant, and it gave off sweet smoke that he watched curl into the air.

"It's called a joss stick," the woman said, knowing he was watching it.

"Joss. It smells good," he said.

"I had a cat named Joss," she said. "A good cat. I don't suppose the name would do for a dog."

"It might," he said. "I could think about it."

"How old are you?" she asked.

"Fourteen," he said. And that was the truth.

Night darkened the windows of the house until he saw the two of them in the separated panes of glass. She was smaller than he was, and careful moving with a thin cap of white hair, and seeing that made him ashamed that he'd forgotten to remove his Broncos hat. He was double ashamed he hadn't asked for her name. It felt too late to do it now.

He said, "I should take this pup and go on."

"Oh," she said, clearing his plate. "You're getting ahead of me. You're making a move, and I haven't even asked you to stay."

The air around him closed in with all its smells, then opened again to his hard breathing. He took Bell onto his lap, not knowing what to say.

She said, "I appreciate your not fooling with me. You have character. I know you're on your own, I can see that much. It's cold out, or it will be, and you need a place to sleep."

He sat in the chair she'd given to him, thinking. There was a bladed feeling in his stomach. He wanted to dull that blade and keep it sharp all at once. After a long minute he asked if she was a schoolteacher.

"I have been a teacher. I've been a lot of things, some of them good, some just necessary. You don't have to worry, I don't ask many questions."

"Just a few."

"A few. Yes."

Bell was wiggling to get down. He stood, planning to walk out.

"The dog," the woman said. "She shouldn't be in that cold without a name or a bed. You need to think of her."

He cleaned himself at her sink and put on a sweatshirt she gave to him. The shirt was soft and faded. He wondered if it belonged to her son. There was a box for Bell with rags and paper. For him, there were blankets the woman brought from downstairs. It looked like she slept there, in the basement. She'd said he could sleep on the floor next to Bell.

"It's not like home," she said.

He said, "It's real nice. Thank you."

"I call it home," she said, seeming to chew around the word. "That's my name for what it's made of me."

After the woman left, Bell lay down in her box, and he sat upright and watched her breathe for a long time. He liked how her body was loose. He liked how the day hadn't left any marks on her. He touched her a few times on the head before he lay down to make himself loose. The house was warm, and it felt smaller than ever, like a tight, lidded box. He wondered if his breath, and Bell's, and the sad, stretched breathing of the woman, could fill up the box in a single night.

They were at the door before he was awake. There was one at first, a deputy, and then another one. He was confused from sleep and from how quickly the woman walked around him and around Bell like she could see fine in the dark. She didn't say anything. It wasn't even morning. Bell shook herself like dogs do. She started licking at her fur with her tongue while the inside of him took off running at full speed, his heart and his head—flying at full speed. The rest of him stayed put, stiff and silent next to Bell. It was too late.

The woman tried to talk to the deputies through her door, but they came in, two of them dressed in uniforms and thick jackets. He stayed on the floor with his legs held straight under the blankets so they could see he'd quit. When one of them said his real name, he nodded. He knew they'd seen copies of his picture.

"You come along with us," the first deputy said. "We know you got a story. We don't want trouble."

He nodded again. Asked if he could put on his shoes.

"Not until we check," the first one said. "Stand up and let us check."

They stood him up and put on handcuffs and took the money from his pockets and took his hat, and while they touched him in those ways, his mind went to a high, cool place where it could stand hours of dark and hours of light and still hear the occasional hopeful words if they were spoken. He knew how to quit. And he knew how not to quit on everything. The thing he would miss most was Bell. He'd really wanted it to work out with her.

The woman was talking faster than her usual talk. With more letters and sharp notes.

She said, "I didn't ask questions. But I know a thing or two, I figured you out."

He stood there wearing her soft sweatshirt, not able to give it back.

She looked at him with padlocked eyes. "It's the kind of person I am. What I've turned into. I made a clear decision."

He asked, "Will you take care of her?"

"I can't."

"I wish you'd thought of her. She likes it here. I guess I don't think it's right not to think of her, a little dog, when you make a decision. That's how you said it with me. You said I had to consider." He remembered how Ray had thrown Bell out of the truck and how he'd never told the woman about that. Maybe it would have made a difference to her, that story.

She said, "You made your decision when you put your father in a pool of blood up there in Lyman. It might have been right to do that. I don't know. Things get out of order in a family. Living gets us out of order."

He climbed upward to his place, hand over hand. The woman went on, and the deputies went on, and they laid out their sentences like smooth, straight roads telling about his sister and who was caring for her and what his chances were. Bell left her box and came to his feet. She scratched at his jeans with her claws until the second deputy picked her up.

He said, "Cute dog."

The woman said, "You let him ride with that dog, Walt Mason. You let him have her in the car for the drive to where you're going. He won't see her again."

He heard what the woman said next to his high, quiet ears. She *had* been a schoolteacher, it was all through her voice. He was glad to know that. She had been a teacher in another time and another world that never included him, maybe a world that worked better than his did. She had taught things he hadn't learned. Still, he knew little Bell would be good for the woman, he felt that, everybody in the tiny house had to feel that, and the woman didn't want the dog. He didn't understand. He would never understand, not with any carving of his heart he wouldn't. How could anybody not want the thing that would keep them from being sent backward one last time?

The Great Cheese

Mason Salisbury and his son, Moreau, were hunting by Little Sandy Creek several miles from where the stream ran through town and powered the Salisbury mill. Father and son carried old fowling pieces and hadn't brought the dogs; they weren't hunting so much as talking. Moreau was home from seminary in Cazenovia. He hadn't wanted to be a miller, and who could argue with a desire to serve God? A father, perhaps, but Mason hadn't. Moreau left Sandy Creek convinced "there was more in heaven and earth than a grist mill." Mason had wondered how much "more" resided in seminary.

"The Latin and Greek drummed into your head will make you a fine preacher," said Mason.

"I'm not a good speaker," said Moreau.

"It'll teach you rhythm. Like the mill. I run sums, Greek, or the words of Shakespeare through my mind. There's a rhythm to stone grinding wheat or corn. You might call it philosophical."

Moreau smiled; more likely the words of Daniel Webster and Senator Seward ran through his father's mind. Mason was a political man. A talker. His son would be different. He would talk to God.

Moreau's life, if he stayed in Sandy Creek, would be work, family, community. He was the only son of a miller, a Baptist in a congregation where not less than forty people were either Salisburys or married to a Salisbury, the richest man in town was married to a Salisbury, and Uncle Lorenzo Salisbury had a large farm down the Salt Road. Moreau feared his life might run as predictably and slowly as the creek moving over the broken layers of limestone and its hundreds of little falls, as Little Sandy wound through town, collected in the mill pond, and flowed to Lake Ontario. So he went to Cazenovia looking for God.

"The way I see it," said Mason, "we'll all miss the sound of that grindstone, and miss it badly."

"War?"

"Yes, war."

Father and son and everybody in town and all the towns in Jefferson and Oswego Counties talked of war. Since the Dred Scott decision when the Supreme Court upheld the Fugitive Slave Act, reaffirming the legality of returning human beings to bondage, Mason felt war was inevitable.

"Slavery is an affront to God." Mason ran his hand down the barrel of a fowling piece that belonged to his father, Reuben, who fought in 1812, and who, with nine other Salisburys, left Vermont for the New York frontier forty-five years before.

"North and South compromised to avoid war," said Moreau.

"That's no compromise," said his father, "but a pact with hell."

Moreau knew his father meant what he said. Mason supported the UGRR, the underground railroad for getting runaway slaves to Canada. From here it was eighty miles north and across the St. Lawrence, or a dangerous fifty across open lake. The main route was through Syracuse to Buffalo and around Niagara Falls, but sometimes tired and frightened men and women came through Sandy Creek, were hidden in the mill among sacks of meal until Mason escorted the fugitives to a lumber boat. Moreau had taken food and clothing into the mill for half-starved men, and once a shivering woman, but he'd never accompanied a runaway to Canada.

Unlike most men in the North Country, Mason Salisbury had seen slavery. He had been south as a young man, and it changed his life.

"Tell about New York and Washington," Moreau said. The story was a ritual between father and son.

Mason leaned back. A black slouch hat protected his face from the sun. He enjoyed telling the story. Moreau enjoyed listening.

It started as a lark—the greatest lark in local history. A neighbor, Colonel Thomas Meacham, was a showman. One might think the difficulties of wrestling a town out of the forests of the North Country, along with the ferocious winters, would freeze a man's imagination the way all three branches of Sandy Creek froze in winter, but Meacham's mind never rested. He built the Agricultural Hall on what became the fairgrounds. He trained the local militia. In 1835 the colonel decided to make a "universal" name for himself and the town. Meacham proposed to make the world's largest cheese and present it to President Andrew Jackson. The

Democrats were delighted, the Whigs thought presenting one cheese to another most appropriate, and cynics, which the North Country produced like oaks, thought the idea would mark Sandy Creek as home to the world's biggest cheese and biggest fool.

The odyssey of Meacham's cheese was the pivotal event in Mason Salisbury's life. Years later, during the winter of 1862, when father and son and uncle, each in solitary agony after Antietam, put a gun to his head, and struggled for a reason not to pull the trigger, Mason traced the chain of events to this trip.

In July Colonel Meacham soaked hickory boards in the creek, bent them around a white oak, and nailed them in a circle to make a gigantic cheese hoop. Meacham made the cheese in the Agricultural Hall, so all could watch. He first removed the permanent exhibits: the only McCormick Reaper north of Albany, a stuffed three-legged chicken, and the *pièce de résistance,* a two-headed calf pickled in brine. The colonel understood imagination is fired by the rational and the outrageous—scientific marvels and freaks of nature. The cheese was the marvel; taking it to Andrew Jackson, outrageous.

The tale was local lore on a par with the Battle of Sandy Creek during the War of 1812, and the subsequent hauling of a nine-thousand-pound ship's cable from Big Sandy to Sackets Harbor on the shoulders of two hundred local men. Moreau had been brought up on these tales, but preferred the cheese saga because it involved Salisburys. He enjoying hearing his father tell it, especially on an unseasonably warm afternoon.

After completing the hoop, Meacham slaughtered four heifers, removed their fourth stomachs—the gastronomically preferred stomach—and soaked the guts in brine until the linings turned into rennet, the ingredient for curdling milk. A giant cheese press took two months to build and looked like a gibbet, except a millstone was lowered from a six-foot arm, not a criminal.

In October the colonel's one hundred fifty cows were milked twice a day, and the milk was poured into oak tubs in the Agricultural Hall. Mason and his brother, Lorenzo, found time to watch. Everybody watched. Whether people thought Meacham the local genius or local fool, the cheese was an event that broke the routine of work and winter. In October, when the poplars blazed yellow along the lake shore and wind ripped down leaves and cut the clear air with cold, Meacham made his cheese. The rennet went in the tubs, and the milk was stirred with long wooden paddles until it curdled. The lumpy liquid was poured through willow baskets leaving curds to be pressed into cheese. After ten days and six thousand gallons of milk, a fourteen-hundred-pound cheese appeared.

The Salisburys were for the colonel. Mason, the talkative one, wanted to go to Washington. He was twenty-six and wanted to meet new people, especially important ones, see new places, especially New York City, and meet women, possibly rich. Mason had secretly dreamed of going to New York City to seek his fortune. Lorenzo, taller, quiet, more interested in how things worked than people or cities, thought making the largest cheese only a matter of degree. He was more interested in how it would be transported. Lorenzo had married in March and didn't wish to leave his bride, even to meet Andrew Jackson.

The cheese looked like an enormous birthday cake. An artist painted pictures of George Washington, Miss Columbia, and eagle medallions on a long paper, which Meacham dubbed "the National Belt," and wrapped around the sides of the cheese. The biggest party ever seen in Sandy Creek was held for the departure. Hogs were slaughtered, lake trout fried, turkeys roasted, tubs of mashed potatoes prepared along with red cabbage slaw, creamed onions, cucumber supreme, sweet pickles, mustard dill, Indian pudding, and gallons of home-brewed ale and sweet cider. Nothing like it would be seen until the Civil War.

The next day, "the Ides of November," Mason quipped, forty-eight gray stallions pulled a sledge carrying the great cheese and eight smaller ones, only seven hundred fifty pounds each, which were to be given to dignitaries along the way. A cannon fired a salute, and a procession a mile long of buggies and swells on their best mounts followed the cheeses down the Salt Road to Pulaski, where flatboats took them to the lake port of Selkirk.

At Pulaski, Mason finished a flask of whiskey and felt the sting of homesickness—being away from home suddenly seemed terribly lonely, even for a man seeking his fortune—when he was tapped on the shoulder. It was Lorenzo. "You ain't goin' alone." Mason hugged his brother and felt Lorenzo's two-hammered, short-stocked shotgun under his long brown coat. It was a nasty weapon, good at close range. Lorenzo came equipped with more than dreams.

A schooner had been engaged to take the cheeses and men to Oswego. A vicious storm blew up after dark, ripping down the forward jib and almost washing Meacham's marvels off the sleet-slicked deck. Neither brother had ever been caught on the lake at night in a storm, let alone a winter storm. Mason prayed on his knees and held on to his bunk. Lorenzo shook his head and went on deck to help secure the cheeses. Mason retched. The next day they laughed, and Lorenzo said, "The lake's a treacherous lady." Mason swore he'd never sail on it at night again. Silently, he swore to never be that afraid again.

At Oswego the cheeses were put on a canal boat. Crowds cheered, and flags flew. Mason was exhilarated. This was a fore-taste of New York City. The men from the North Country were hailed by city folk. Ladies waved handkerchiefs. Gents threw hats in the air. The Sandy Creek men and cheeses went down the Oswego River to the Oswego Canal, then to Syracuse, where the colonel had a sign nailed to the boat—*Meacham's Mighty Marvel The Eighth Wonder of the World*—and bigger crowds cheered the *Brian Boru* as it entered the Erie Canal. Lorenzo was fascinated by the canal. He talked to everyone onboard from the captain to the sweepers about speed, depth, locks, length of journey, even pirates, and agreed the canal was the "eighth wonder of the world." Mason thought New York City was the eighth wonder, and sometimes wondered if he himself might not be the ninth. The steady pace of the packet, interrupted by wildly enthusiastic crowds, was conducive to dreaming. The brothers pondered the significance of the canal. Lorenzo was impressed by the locks and how the canal had been cut through hills. Mason watched the traffic going east-west and thought of all the commerce starting, ending, or passing through New York City. Gotham was indeed the seat of fortune.

Lorenzo was prescient to ask about pirates. The Canal was new, and the men who worked it rough. Buffalo, New York, had the highest murder rate in the country. "Canawlers" finishing the trip from Albany drank, whored, fought, and often found the end of life's journey with a crushed skull at the bottom of their beloved "canawl." Near Troy, two hundred fifty miles west, was the

"Bloody Cut," a hotbed for gangs looking for fights and loot between jobs.

Moreau and his father sat under a tall oak. Mason watched a patch of thick underbrush by a cluster of willows, oaks, and tag alders by the creek. The fowling pieces rested against a log. Moreau had heard the tale so often, thought about it so much, retold and imagined it, that it was both history and a guide to the future. Young men should travel, be tested, and had to leave the North Country to do so.

"I wish I'd been there," Moreau said. It was the son's way of saying what wouldn't be said overtly. "I wish I'd been with you."

"It was an adventure."

Mason had been twenty-six. Lorenzo twenty-five. They'd been brought up on tales of 1812, when Sackets Harbor was the most important ship building port on the Great Lakes and local men ambushed the British at Big Sandy. Mason's generation hadn't gotten a war. He often lamented the fact. War had come in Texas where a hundred eighty men in an old mission would find immorality in death, but in 1835 a Sandy Creek man needed imagination to be noticed.

"I wish I had reason to go somewhere," said Moreau.

"That's the way I felt."

"A man needs to wander," said Moreau. "Do new things."

"Things he wouldn't tell anyone?" said his father.

"What makes you say that?"

"I felt it."

When the *Brian Boru* tied up near Troy shortly after dusk, men appeared. A one-eyed man climbed on the gangway. Lorenzo had heard about Patch Malone, leader of the roughest gang in the "Cut." Colonel Meacham, in a black frock coat and high beaver hat, leapt to the top of the gangway and shouted, "This cargo is for President Jackson!" Mason froze. He thought of himself as a talker, not a fighter, but was speechless. He reached for Lorenzo, who didn't talk or fight much but was capable of both. Lorenzo moved up behind Meacham. A man with Malone struck a lucifer and lit a torch, which was passed around, and a dozen torches flared, filling gangway, dock, and deck with lurid shadows as the brands were raised and lowered in unison. Mason, not moving, hot fear in his throat, watched. He saw a man missing an ear, counted fourteen unshaven rascals, noticed pistols and knives in belts, broken teeth, toothless gaps in grins, and was mesmerized by the glittering single eye of Patch Malone.

"Jackson ain't here," said Malone.

"Stand clear!" ordered Meacham. Shadows ominously rose and fell over gangway, deck, and men.

"Share the cheese, you damned dandy."

"Not with the likes of you!"

"Too good for Irishmen, are ye?"

Lorenzo was directly behind Colonel Meacham, so the irregular light and leaping shadows didn't reveal the contours of the weapon under the brown coat, or perhaps Malone was carried away with audacity and liquor.

"We ain't Democrats! We're Whigs!" shouted Patch Malone, to the delight of his followers.

"Whigs! Whigs!" yelled the torch-bearers.

"You're scoundrels!" said Meacham.

Malone swaggered up the gangway. "I like that hat!" Malone reached for Meacham's topper, and Lorenzo Salisbury did to Patch Malone what Hernán Cortés did to Montezuma—took him hostage, sticking both barrels into Patch's stomach and saying, "I'm aimin' lower." Lorenzo yanked the one-eyed man onto the deck and then pulled back each brass hammer. Each clicked menacingly.

"Tell your men to get away from the boat."

Malone looked at the gun and turned his head. "Back, men."

The gangway was pulled up, and the *Brian Boru* untied. As the packet departed, Meacham pushed Patch Malone overboard.

Even as a child, Moreau thought the moral of that episode wasn't the gun, quick-thinking, or courage, but some men are believed when they say they'll shoot you; others aren't. Moreau didn't think he was one of those believed. Or his father. Uncle Lorenzo was another matter.

At Albany, Colonel Meacham gave cheeses to Governor Marcy and the legislature. The boat and its cargo were cheered by hundreds waving flags, hats, and handkerchiefs. A few carried signs supporting President Jackson and lauding the cheese. Mason noticed people of all variety: mechanics, stout wives, lanky farmers, gentlemen in fine coats, ladies in fur, young girls who squealed and kissed each other, gawky boys who made faces, pinched girls, or threw a stone and ran. The North Country men were toasted by assemblymen and senators in black coats as shiny and worn as the colonel's. Mason thought giving toasts and speeches was a far cry from milling and wondered what it took to stand for office. There was a world elsewhere. Mason looked at his gabardine trousers, rough shirt, and patched coat, and wondered if he had enough money to buy new clothes in New York. A man ought to look a certain way.

The *Brian Boru* entered the Hudson River, and Mason had never seen anything as majestic as the cliffs, towering trees, wide river, and constant traffic. All water, he told Lorenzo, leads to New York. One could go from Lake Superior to London or Africa or China. Water was the road to the world, and they were on it.

"I've never seen anything so beautiful."

"I'll take Lake Ontario," said Lorenzo.

Both men were awed by the broad river as it passed under the promontories of West Point and sluiced through the Storm King Gap. Even in cold, gray December, they felt the genteel richness of the Hudson Valley. This was life backed by money and families who'd been here two hundred years. Mason wanted to live here— either in this patrician valley where winter didn't bury cabins, next to water that wouldn't kill you, or in the city rising at the mouth of the mighty Hudson. Any fool could see this was the gateway to the world. Lorenzo thought Mason saw what Mason wanted to see. This was nothing new, and Lorenzo kept his opinion to himself.

Neither Salisbury had ever been farther than Oswego. They weren't prepared for Lower Manhattan Island. The farms, trees, and roads of the upper island seemed a civilized use of marvelously situated land, but as the river got more crowded with side-wheelers belching wood-smoke, packets, schooners, barges, merchantmen, sloops, yachts braving the December river—and the shore such a continuous line of spars, rigging, and hulls a man might walk around the tip of Manhattan without touching land or water—they saw and smelled the City of New York.

Mason noted they arrived on the Ides of December, a full month out of the North Country. "Another fateful day," he told his brother.

At Coenties Slip on the East River, the *Brian Boru* was met by Bushrod T. Hawkins, a Manhattan Meacham, and proprietor of Hawkins' American Museum on Pearl Street. Hawkins had a sleigh, reporters, and a crowd waiting. The sleigh was covered with red, white, and blue bunting, and a sign trumpeted the arrival of the world's biggest cheese. After listening to speeches and watching the crowd, which hooted, winked, laughed, threw hats in the air, and loudly cheered Andrew Jackson, the brothers decided this wasn't a place to be clapped on the back and bought a drink by a stranger. "I ain't part of no show," Lorenzo said, and the Salisburys ventured into Manhattan by themselves.

They walked Pearl Street, taking in the maze of new wooden buildings that seemed to have sprung up on every available patch of land. Lorenzo commented on that particularly New York street mix of men with nothing to do and men in a devil of a hurry. Mason admitted the place was huge and filthy. They both thought the natives either looked too closely or paid you no attention. Lorenzo, gun under his long coat, wondered how so many people could live so close together without killing each other. He was told they frequently did. The brothers stopped for a nickel glass of beer and accompanying free lunch—bad cheese on bad bread—in a place with sawdust on the floor and grimy pictures of race-horses and prizefighters, including Tom Molineaux, ex-Virginian slave turned British pugilist, on the walls. Mason confided to Lorenzo he was thinking of seeking his fortune in New York, and Lorenzo replied, "I feared so." Mason realized his brother had left his bride to keep Mason from leaving the North Country, and was deeply touched. He took his brother's arm when they walked out.

Neither Salisbury liked the hovels of the poor, the masses of people, especially the forlorn young girls selling corn from baskets. They had never seen garbage in the streets, dealt with only by free-ranging pigs, dead horses left to stink and decay, so many low, smoky doggeries full of men, or the rabbit warren of narrow, crooked mercantile streets, but there was energy. There was, at least for Mason, the grit and anonymity—the feeling anything can happen, right now, and nobody will know—that frightened and intrigued strangers in New York. Lorenzo said he was glad he was married; Mason was glad he wasn't. They went to the district where unaccompanied women appeared after dark. How Mason knew about the Bowery wasn't clear, but they *had* been on a boat for a month. Mason told Lorenzo it was the best area for a cheap dinner. Lorenzo said, "For sure." Of all possible pleasures of the night, the brothers settled for root beer at three cents a glass. Mason was cautious, Lorenzo was mindful of Mason, so it was enough to eat sausage, drink root beer, and walk streets that ended at docks full of hard-looking men and dark river cluttered with spars and rigging.

Whatever might have happened with con men, corn girls, unaccompanied women, or the host of canny Manhattan folk who emerged after dark—the potential comedy or disaster of Yankee jakes negotiating the Bowery—was cut short by the night of the sixteenth. Mason's facetious foreboding about the Ides of November and December came wildly true. Fire broke out around nine p.m. Sheets of flame rose over the tall dry goods and hardware stores on Merchant Street and raced through the district incinerating hovels, factories, doggeries, even the Stock Exchange. In fifteen minutes, fifty buildings were on fire. Then all structures, brick, stone, wood—warehouse, office, or church—were burning. The temperature was near zero. It was snowing. A nor'wester cut the city with sleet, ice, driving snow. Wells and cisterns froze. Fireman, exhausted from fighting a large fire at Burling's Slip the previous day, and decimated by cholera the previous summer, were slow to arrive. When they did, most hydrants were frozen; when hoses sprayed, water froze into hail. The wind blew so hard the East River was flattened and suction hoses couldn't reach the water. It was disaster worthy of any country parson's Gomorrahic vision of New York.

Moreau loved the story. It was raw adventure. He frequently imagined his father and uncle getting through the panic of passersby, terrified horses, flaming buildings. "We thought the sky was on fire," Mason said. Moreau could see them running by singed teams straining to pull stuck fire wagons, dodging frightened citizens and squealing pigs, skirting dead horses. For a boy in freezing Sandy Creek, the vision of a world on fire and his father and uncle negotiating blazing streets, barely able to

breathe, strangers in the city, saints in hell, was absolute vindica-
tion of the North Country and a terrific adventure. It was what
Moreau chafed for now.

"Were you scared?" Moreau asked.

"No time to be scared. Or maybe I was so scared, I didn't notice.
We ran through that inferno, and I knew I couldn't ever live there.
Not in that place. We were cured like hams in a smokehouse."

Fire raged across Lower Manhattan. The Salisburys raced down
Pearl Street to Hawkins' American Museum.

"We come with the cheese!" Lorenzo shouted. "By God we'll
leave with it!"

The wind was at their backs pushing the fire, filling the street
with cinders and smoke. The brothers reached the building and
found the colonel. Meacham put horse blankets over the cheese,
and the three men had to carry it to a sleigh. Back home it took
eleven men and a cheering crowd, but this wasn't home.

Moreau looked at the thick grove of willows and oaks by the
creek. Something moved, but Moreau preferred his father's tale to
tramping out a pheasant or rousting a grouse. He looked at the
old man—white beard, hard muscles, alert eyes—and wondered
what the young man had been like. Who was that man who left
Sandy Creek to do things he wouldn't tell anyone? There was a
restlessness about Mason now, so uncharacteristic of the North
Country, a willingness to engage anyone in talk on any subject,
though the subject invariably became abolition. Moreau knew his
father had been tested. Tested in the big city. What a gift, he
thought, provided you survived. That was the great thing about
the cheese story. The teller had been there and survived.

Moreau stretched in the afternoon sun and wondered what he
had to tell. Was it this story, or the tale of two hundred men carrying a four-ton cable twenty miles? They were wonderful stories,
but they weren't his story. Moreau believed sometime in a man's
life he would be asked to do the impossible. Maybe he could or
maybe he couldn't, but he would be asked. No one ever told
Moreau this, but he fervently believed it. His father did the
impossible—even if it was for a cheese. Moreau knew the tale had
been polished, nuances adjusted, and lessons embedded in the

narrative. Had his father really been ready to move to New York? If the brothers had arrived any day but December 15, 1835, would Moreau be a city slicker, raised in Manhattan? Would the Salisburys be rich? Would Moreau be a clerk in a high-backed chair with a mean, long-nosed boss? The story put the virtues of Sandy Creek in clear relief. Maybe too clear, but Moreau loved it. He wanted to see the sky on fire and dash through hell. If the Apocalypse wasn't available, a long trip might do.

The men got the cheese to the sleigh. Under ordinary circumstances this would have been miraculous, but in the midst of a fire that would burn for sixteen hours and destroy 693 buildings, nothing was ordinary. The colonel and the two Salisburys dragged the cheese off its pedestal—it was not destined for a long New York run—and hauled it out as the museum roof caught fire. The brothers hung on to cheese and sleigh as Meacham whipped the horses, and they flew down Pearl Street. Sparks went over their heads, burned the horses, danced in red air. "The devil don't drive faster!" Lorenzo yelled. Mason looked back and saw the American Museum go up as they dashed for the river. Smoke choked the streets; cinders burned pedestrians. Horses reared. They saw a fire wagon turn over at the corner of Water Street.

"Fire follows sin!" Meacham yelled.

"We ain't sinned yet!" shouted Lorenzo.

The sleigh bounced over debris, slipped on ice, skidded on frozen ruts, splashed through freezing water. The red, white, and blue bunting, the National Belt, ripped. The brothers dug their hands into cheese and managed to keep fourteen hundred pounds and themselves on the sleigh. It wasn't for nothing they had grown up hauling sacks of grain and meal.

Moreau liked thinking of his father and uncle hurling through New York City's worst fire, up to their elbows in cheese, rushing through flame, sparks, and falling debris. Whoever heard of anything so wonderful? The lessons were clear: heroism is expected; survival is purchased with courage.

A son invents his father out of such tales.

Within sight of the *Brian Boru* straining at its mooring but untouched by spark or flame, they heard a ferocious crack. The heat was so intense, Mason thought the air had exploded. "Look out!" Lorenzo shouted. A church steeple teetered: cinders and flame shot hundreds of feet in the air.

They didn't have time to jump.

The colonel whipped the team. The story could have ended in the ruins of Pearl Street in sight of the canal packet, providing fodder for generations of North Country sermons on town *hubris* and city peril, but the horses found an extra burst. The steeple came down in a plume of sparks, glowing wood, and rushing flame. It grazed the sleigh's tailgate.

They made the dock, loaded the cheese, and the packet pulled out into the East River.

"What the hell good are churches, anyway?" Lorenzo said.

The brothers saw slaves in Maryland. Neither had seen one before. In Baltimore, slaves unloaded freight and sang carols with a melancholy intensity, not easily forgotten. Mason wondered if this familiar yet strange sound was a sign, but decided a sign should be more dramatic.

No crowds greeted the cheese in Washington. People at the station were more interested in the disaster in New York. Christmas in the capital was a muddy, lonely affair. Everyone, it seemed, had somewhere else to be. The city was a disappointment. The roads were unpaved and the buildings so far apart fire wasn't a threat. Mason said Washington was a muddy idea for a city. "A hope and a plan. December must not be the best month." Lorenzo wondered how populated the city might become. Colonel Meacham was informed President Jackson, though appreciative of the cheese, was too sick to meet the North Country men.

The city of mud and damp cold offered no dazzling parties, connections, or rich widows. A slave did tip his hat and say, "Welcome, cheese men," as Meacham's fourteen hundred pounds disappeared into the back of the White House, but the colonel and his party were not the celebrities they had been in Syracuse and Albany. Meacham was miserable. The day before they left the nation's capital, with its few scattered impressive buildings, indifferent hotels, infamous boarding houses, provided Mason his sign.

Mason had stopped looking for signs. He was trying to shake a cough and congestion brought on by the cold in New York and damp of Washington. He was ready to go home to warmer fires, tell everyone New York City was dirty and crowded even when not on fire, and visit a young woman who had been most sorry to see him go.

On Christmas Day, Mason and Lorenzo walked the deserted streets, viewed the long, open expanses between buildings, and wished they were home.

"I'm not impressed," Mason said.

Lorenzo shook his head. "It ain't the Erie Canal."

"It ain't even Albany," said Mason.

The brothers passed an empty pen that seemed small for cattle. A post equipped with chains revealed its use.

"Slaves," said Lorenzo.

"At least they don't buy and sell human beings in the capital of the world's only democracy on the birthday of the Savior," said Mason.

They walked towards the White House and considered stopping to inquire about the President's health. The day was gray and cold, though walking in the damp air felt less chilly than their drafty boarding house. The Salisburys were wearing their long coats, and Lorenzo had his short-stocked shotgun.

They passed a whitewashed boarding house, a place more in need of repair than their own lodgings, and heard screams and the sound of a whip. They went around back to a stable, where a heavy man, his white collarless shirt stained with sweat, lashed a Negro. The Negro stood on an unpainted stool, hands tied together and hung over a rusty hook in a joist. His neck, shoulders, back, and feet were bare. His shiny black back was bloody, and his ragged pants were bright with blood. Three stable hands passed a jug. "Put your back into it, John," said one. They wore soiled shirts with the sleeves rolled up. Mason saw everything in an instant, as if daguerreotype images were imprinted on his memory. A white mark on the forehead of a horse in a stall. The gap between the blackened teeth of the man swigging out of the jug. Rakes and bridles on the walls. A saddle in a pile of straw. The upraised hoof of a gray horse in a stall. A lantern on a chest whose varnished top was cracked. The crease in a slouch hat in the straw beside John. Manure on John's boots. The kind of whip called a cowhide. And most of all, red welts, blood flowing on the Negro's shiny back, muscles and tendons stretched so they might break. Bloody feet on tiptoe on the rough stool.

The brothers stood in the door. Lorenzo put his hand under his coat.

"You got business?" said John. He spat.

The Salisburys didn't answer.

"It costs to watch a cow hidin'," said the man with the jug.

"A quarter."

"That ain't enough," said a squat man with big forearms and bulging stomach, who leaned against a stall.

The Salisburys looked at each other.

John gave the Negro two hard lashes and grunted with the effort. He evidently enjoyed inflicting pain. The Negro turned, and Mason saw his face by the light of the lantern. The face was old, helpless, begging. Blood ran down the man's bare feet and dripped on the stool. He screamed. John hit him again.

Mason was humiliated, fascinated, and furious. He couldn't watch; he couldn't not watch. He felt the raw satisfaction of the stable hands. They guffawed and swigged. He felt the hot arrogance of cruelty in John. The vicious pride. Mason again stood before men. He took off his coat, walked over straw, by the hat, lantern, John, the whip. He put his coat over the man's bloody shoulders. The coat covered him to the ankles.

"Damn waste of a good coat," said John, and spat in the straw.

"He's cold," said Mason.

"Yankees," said a stable hand.

"Yankees don't know niggers," said another.

"Don't know nothin'."

"He's cold," said Mason.

"Thank him," said John, touching the Negro's ear with the whip.

Tears ran down the black man's face. He looked old. Old enough to be their father.

Lorenzo was behind Mason. Coat unbuttoned.

"Get out," said John.

"Do you call yourself a Christian?" said Mason, looking John in the eye.

The whip made a stinging sound and peremptory crack as it hit Mason across the face. Mason doubled over, clutching his face. Lorenzo hit John along the side of the head with the barrel of the shotgun and in the stomach with the butt. John staggered and sat down in the straw. The whip dropped. John put his hand to his head, which was bleeding, and groaned.

A stable hand reached for a pitchfork. Another picked up a rake.

"Don't," said Lorenzo. It was the voice he used in the "Bloody Cut."

No one moved.

Mason said, "Give me the gun."

"No," said Lorenzo.

The Negro sobbed like a child. The sound was unbearable.

"I'll kill him," said Mason. A red mark ran from Mason's cheek to his hairline.

"It's his country," said Lorenzo, moving back, gun leveled at John.

Mason stepped on the hat. "For now."

The brothers walked out of the stable. Mason didn't look back. Lorenzo didn't take his eye off the men.

The Salisburys kept walking. They heard the whip and screams louder than before. Mason didn't feel the cold.

He'd never been so hot.

Sleepwalk

Maybe the whole thing could be accounted for by the year, 1971: how we—well, I—woke at three in the morning with a funny sensation that something, somebody, was missing, and wandered out to the living room where my childhood sweetheart, the love-of-my-life Richie, was supposed to be sleeping on the couch. He was gone. He hadn't even shut the door all the way. I leaned out the front window and caught sight of him crossing Broadway between 106th and 107th, jaywalking behind a *Daily News* delivery truck in his bare feet. He was naked except for his underwear, white huggies with holes in back I could see even from six flights up.

Thank God it was spring: a warm spring, almost a year since Kent State and nine months since the draft lottery for guys born in 1951. Richie was number 37, which meant he had to either stay in school or ship out to Vietnam, but he'd got himself tangled up in some Weathermen business. Now he was on the lam—or so he had told us a few hours before, over a bowl of chili. It was hard to say exactly how much beer we'd drunk at that point: he and Jean-Paul kept popping up to go buy another bottle of Miller High Life, the pair of them insisting, *No, man, it's on me.* Mainly they wanted to put some distance between each other. All guys were like that, I thought then, like the city dogs you'd see on the sidewalk or in Riverside Park, shepherds and huskies on little leather leads, their owners holding them back when another dog passed and hissing, *Is he male? Is he male? Cause if he's male…*

If he's male, my dog'll go for blood, and here's fair warning. Well, we had no warning from Richie. He just rang the buzzer downstairs, and the next thing I knew he was at the apartment door, the two of us hugging and bawling. Jean-Paul wasn't home yet, and Richie bent his knees to get down to my height and rub up against me the way he used to do when we were fourteen and fifteen and sixteen. I half-wanted him to make all the other moves, too, the tongue in my mouth and the one-handed breast squeeze, but he didn't, he just held on for dear lustful life.

"Twenty years old, Feeney? Frigging married? Where's the little tyke?"

"Richie, I wasn't pregnant. That's not the only reason people get married." With his breath on my neck, though, I couldn't remember what the other reasons were. Jean-Paul and I had been planning to move in together, but my father had lung cancer in a bad way and my mother said she'd slam the door in my face if I showed up, unwed and cohabitating, to visit him. So while the rest of the world cavorted in communes, here we were in a minuscule claustrophobic apartment, lawfully wed.

And here was Richie, his hair tied back with a shoelace and his sleeves rolled to his elbows. Over the fifth or sixth quart of beer he asked Jean-Paul—not me—if he could crash: "We got a safe house lined up in Brooklyn. Park Slope, man, a duplex this chick is renting for us, only the owner's sniffing around. Two days, maybe three? I'd really appreciate it."

"Must be weird to be back in New York," Jean-Paul said, non-committal. He didn't like the Weather Underground, and he didn't like the idea of the feds showing up at our door.

"Dig it. But I couldn't stay in Madison with this shit going down. Cozy in my safe little *school* with Kissinger napalming every country in Southeast Asia?" Richie wasn't the least concerned about insulting those of us who'd stayed in our safe little schools. We still didn't know exactly what he'd done, but when I leaned in to ask, Jean-Paul signaled with his eyebrows to keep still: the less we knew the better. He was probably right.

"Just don't go blowing anybody up." I pictured the front page of the *News* when they blew up that townhouse in the Village: a nail bomb, and three of them dead. *Rich kids,* Jean-Paul said.

Richie could be pretty reckless, but now he gave me his Agony in the Garden look. "We look at every action from every angle, man. I guess there's not a lotta politics in a theater department."

"There's enough," Jean-Paul said. The truth was, he was the most political guy I knew, but he was full of contempt for the hotheads who said they were going out to smash up the Bank of America: the Richies. *You watch,* he always said. *They'll be working for the Bank of America ten years from now.*

"We've been doing some good street theater," I said, but even to me it sounded like my little-girl voice.

PLOUGHSHARES

"Oh, wow," Richie snorted. "Street theater."

Jean-Paul was glowering by then. Richie was a ballplayer—a pitcher, tall and muscular—and he was a talker, a snorter, a stand-up guy who'd just walked away from his Wisconsin scholarship to get messed up in whatever he was messed up in. He didn't have a lot of patience for the Jean-Pauls of the world, and the Jean-Pauls—the ones who went on the marches but wouldn't smash the windows—always looked like they were trying to figure out if they could take him down. The answer was: no. Jean-Paul was dark and intense and good-looking, the lead in the last three main-stage productions, but his hair was cut short for *Waiting for Lefty* and he was skinnier than I was. Next to Richie, next to those big biceps and the big nose and the big mouth, he looked a little nebbishy and sour. He was 4-F: a heart murmur.

"Sure, you can stay," he said. "I'm going out for another quart."

"Champagne of bottle beers," Richie said, and grinned, and hoisted his jelly jar. "Thanks, man." Jean-Paul didn't grin back.

Five years later we moved to Brooklyn ourselves. Back then, when you could still afford it, Park Slope was the destination for all the refugees, all the failed artists and actors and opera singers, and it was crawling with radicals, too. Even before I got pregnant I had a lot of downtime to wander, to search for Richie in the health food store and the big library at Grand Army Plaza and on the ball fields in Prospect Park. I looked all the time, at any tall swarthy male, and for a while I started to see him behind beards and under yarmulkes and once, even, beneath a Sikh turban. I bought every Bruce Springsteen album, to study the pictures, because Bruce had the same moves as Richie, and I had an idea they'd age the same way. Every time I heard a siren in the night, I saw FBI agents cornering him, pulling him away from his new life as a social worker or a labor organizer. Sometimes the last thing I saw before I fell asleep was Richie behind prison bars, Springsteening to imaginary music.

He wasn't in Park Slope anymore, or I would have seen him. I would have known him even if he'd had plastic surgery or dressed as a circus clown. He was probably up on some farm in New Hampshire or out in the Northwest working a fishing trawler. When they started finding people in the nineties—Sara Jane what's her name—I held my breath. I knew what I was doing. Dreaming about Richie, fixating on him, was the safest fantasy a long-married mother of three could possibly have, and anyway I only used the idea of him when Jean-Paul and I were so sick of each other we could spit, or kill each other, or both. Then I'd start looking all over again: he was the one, my grand passion, my Heathcliff, my Vronsky, my roll-me-over Romeo, my Cool Hand Luke. As long as he hadn't blown anybody up. I bought every book on the last days of the SDS to look for his name, but after September 11th I couldn't even turn the pages. Anyway, I never found his name.

But I found him, one rush-hour morning when I wasn't looking at all. He was way down at the front end of the subway platform, the Manhattan-bound D train, wearing a well-cut suit. Very well-cut: Armani, maybe. It could have been a million prosperous guys, and it could only have been him. I moved down the platform for a better look, but the train pulled in and I only had time to focus on a manicured left hand, holding the door for a woman in a tight skirt. No wedding ring—but then Jean-Paul and I didn't wear wedding rings, either, because the ones we bought in the Village were so cheap they split the first time we slammed our hands down in anger. My shortness of breath alarmed me.

I began to see flashes of him everywhere: in the Key Food if I ran in for a quart of milk, coming out of Ozzie's with a cup of coffee. He was always dashing away—avoiding me? Still hiding? I was sure it was Richie. That nose, and the same wavy hair, graying and receding now, but scissor-cut, feathered, long on the neck. An expensive haircut, and an expensive suit, more of a disguise than a Sikh turban. I mean, the Richie Daccapo I knew tied his hair back with a piece of dirty string.

The Richie Daccapo I knew lived next door on Long Island, in Hicksville (no kidding), and when we were five and six and seven you couldn't have pried us apart with the Jaws of Life. I don't even remember going to school when I was that age, I only remember running with Richie out to the hot empty fields where I stood with my wooden bat, pretending I might actually hit the ball, while Richie threw faster and faster and I swung late every time. We were six-year-old lovers, more in tune with each other than anybody who's ever passed through the dark night of puberty.

Not that it was sexless: it was all sex, pulling down shorts behind rhododendron bushes to show each other body parts and touch them and maybe even kiss them: the taste of salt, the smell of my mother's Clorox. When she threw me into the tub at night she snapped, *Don't touch yourself, don't touch your body. What have you been learning from that boy?*

My mother called the Daccapos *coarse:* the *language.* Their *friggings* floated through the patio doors, and Richie's father wore a sleeveless undershirt—how coarse could you get? Actually it was one of the few fashion differences between him and my father, who had, by coincidence, also gone to Fordham night school. Now they were numbers guys (Mr. Daccapo an accountant, Mr. Feeney an actuary), steady faithful family guys who rose at five-thirty to catch the six-forty-five. They always had a pack of cigarettes within hand's reach (Winstons for Feeney, Marlboros for Daccapo), the Zippos lying on top. Richie alternated whose lighter he stole.

We were the gang leaders, Billy the Kid and Pocahontas, hiding in small places, clinging to each other. *Where's my frigging lighter?* Our fathers lay on their couches, dead men listening to Huntley-Brinkley and cough cough coughing, thick yellow phlegm, exhausted worn-out coughs. We crouched between the couch and the wall, squeezing each other, squeezing the Zippo. Maybe we already knew they weren't going to make it. Richie's father dropped dead of a heart attack on the Long Island Railroad when he was forty-four years old. Five years later, my father went in for the chest x-rays.

I can see Mr. Daccapo out in the backyard, the dark hair lush under his arms. He's standing by his new gas grill, his altar, one hand on the cover as if to assure himself that it's all his, or maybe to give it a secret blessing. I'm ashamed to look at him. He just stands there in the dead center of the yard, touching his grill, blissed out. Finally he lifts his hand to shake a Marlboro from the pack and tear the filter off. He's a goner.

I had to shake Jean-Paul awake—all that beer—and when I said Richie was down on Broadway just about naked, gonna get himself killed, he looked at me with that blank look he had already perfected. I said: "Okay, okay, I'll go myself, only don't yell at me if somebody drops a bottle on my head." The Upper West Side still had SROs on every block, and the winos dropped their empties out the windows. My mother couldn't believe we lived like that.

"I'll go," he said, in that male-dog voice, that low flat growl that says *I'll go* and means *and if I catch up with him I'll kill him while I'm at it.*

I watched from the front window, but soon enough Jean-Paul slipped from sight, jogging east. I was surprised to see him running: I thought he'd just walk around the block once and come back to say Richie was long gone. At this hour even Broadway was deserted, open season for the muggers.

After forever the two of them came back into the frame of the window, Richie stooping, trying to hide his tall nakedness behind short Jean-Paul. My guilty little heart beat hard. We'd only been married five months, and already I was comparing one body to the other.

Richie was wild-eyed when he came through the door in his underwear, exhilarated, drunker than when he'd gone to bed drunk. "This guy frigging saved my skin." He put an arm around Jean-Paul's neck, but Jean-Paul picked it off: a bug, a louse. "Your old man hauled off and hit me."

"Somebody had to stop you. Where'd you think you were going?"

Richie collapsed on the couch, groaned, and laughed till something came out of his nose. "I have no frigging idea. Listen, man, thanks for coming after me. Cause if they picked you up with me ..."

We were all wide awake, taking that in. Richie pulled on jeans over his holey BVDs. With his hair down and just the one lamp on, he looked younger than he had all night, maybe a little panicked. "And Feeney, thank God you knew what the deal was—she ever tell you about her sleepwalking days? She was famous for it, man. She used to make *tracks.* She used to wanna get out of town."

It was true. I did make tracks: I ran for my life. I'd wake in a sandlot circling the bases, my parents' robes flapping behind me. They screwed bigger and bigger chains higher and higher on the front door, but no chain could hold me: I dragged a stool over, and I busted out of stir. Someone always heard the scrape across the floor, someone always tore downstairs after me, but always too late, always a swing behind. I was gone, I was out of there.

I was eight, nine, ten those sleepwalking years, the years when the gang split in two, when some of the boys could actually hit Richie's pitches and I was stuck with the girls and their pointy-breasted Barbies. My mother didn't understand why I punished my dolls with needles and buried them up to their necks. Next door Richie and his men put all their green toy soldiers in the new grill with firecrackers and watched them pop-pop-pop, privates gooing all over the rack: excellent practice for the militant wing of the SDS. That night we heard Mr. Daccapo *frigfrigfrig*ing at the top of his lungs, and once we saw him chase Richie down the street with a broom, Richie's voice rising and falling and cracking, a little sob at the end when his father caught up with him.

"I get it," Richie said. "For sure. I'm in Feeney's pad, I associate Feeney with sleepwalking, I sleepwalk myself."

"I'll put the chain on." I knew a chain wouldn't hold Richie, either, but when it was safe in its slot he closed his eyes.

Jean-Paul and I crept back to the little bedroom. "You really hit him?" Under the sheets, we lay a million miles apart.

"You're lucky I didn't strangle him."

The second time he left I heard him rattle the chain, just the way my parents used to hear me, but I was too late. The elevator was already whirring, and Jean-Paul's shoes were already tied. He headed for the stairwell without a goodbye, as if he held me responsible for this sleepwalk of Richie's. Maybe I was.

This time I wasn't staying behind. I slipped into sneakers that had long since lost their laces and took off after them. I was wearing what I wore day and night in 1971: an Indian bedspread I'd scooped out and tied around my neck, no bra in the daytime, and no panties at night. In the dark of night, I could get arrested, too.

I had no idea which way they'd gone so I followed a hunch and headed south on Broadway. At 105th I thought maybe I saw them on the east side of the street, two guys trucking along one after the other. I broke into a noisy run, my loose shoes slapping the sticky sidewalk. It was a cool twitchy muggy night. Broadway smelled of rotting vegetables. The harder I ran, the harder it was to breathe, but up ahead Jean-Paul had almost caught up to Richie, and I had almost caught up to the pair of them.

I put on one last push, but as soon as I was within reach I spied a cop hanging out at the top of the subway stairs across 96th Street. I slowed to a walk just as Richie, barefoot and bare-chested, his pants sliding down his hips and his hair frizzing out, walked right up to the cop and clasped him on the shoulder. Was he awake? Was he turning himself in?

I thought that Jean-Paul would turn around then, but he was a steady faithful guy and he never missed a stride. Crossing 96th, he followed Richie right up to the cop and put his own arm around Richie's shoulder. From my shadow I could make out a pale wary hand flexing on a nightstick.

They stood there forever. I planned my run back home, my calls to find a lawyer for the fugitive and his accomplice. My mother would die. I hadn't said a real prayer since eighth grade, but I heard myself chant *Hail Mary* three times, fast. Lo and behold, the cop swept Richie and Jean-Paul down the street with both hands and then sauntered away.

I reversed course, shamed that I hadn't gone to back up Jean-Paul, and scooted from shadow to shadow till they caught up with me. Then we walked home together after all, wordless till we crossed 105th and Richie keened: "What am I frigging doing? What is this, like a death march?"

"*Death march* is a little melodramatic. Let's just shut up till we're back inside."

We didn't even talk on the elevator. Inside, the door safely latched, Jean-Paul enunciated every word as if Richie were hard of hearing or stupid or both: "What we're going to do is we're going to pile stuff in front of the door." He got to work on a fortress of books and LPs while Richie and I sat stunned on the couch. Pretty soon he had most of our worldly possessions blocking Richie's path. He topped off the pile with the banged-up pots and pans from his father's restaurant, to clang out if Richie got anywhere close.

Richie still didn't look fully conscious. "Time is it, four-thirty? I better sit up, man. How could I do that, go looking for a pig?"

"You don't have to sit up. You're not getting out of here." Jean-Paul played the line just right, world-weary, and exited for the bedroom.

Richie let a long shudder run the length of his body and picked

up my hand to lay it on his chest, so I could feel his heart gallop-
ing. Then he leaned his head back into the cushions and pulled
me close. He tripped his fingers through my hair, curling it strand
by strand the way he used to when we sat on the back steps. Our
breathing slowed, our breathing sped up.

"What did you say to him?"

"The cop? I said *Peace, baby.* Your *husband* told him I was a
frigging frat boy at Columbia who had too much to drink."

"Just don't go blowing anybody up, Richie." I snuggled into
him the way I used to all those afternoons after his father died
and we sat out back trying to make sense of the world.

"Feeney, Feeney." I felt myself melt onto him. "What if I have a
frigging breakdown? What if you have to take me to the emergency room?" I could feel more than his heart rising. He took my
hand to lay it on his jeans, on his doggy cockiness. He wasn't so
scared after all.

From the bedroom the springs squealed: Jean-Paul shifting on
the mattress. Only the little kitchen separated us. He could hear
every word Richie groaned out, and every word I answered. I
jumped up and made my way back to our bed without another
word. It was as if I were sleepwalking, too, only this time I came
back home, locked myself in safe and sound, and nobody even
knew I'd gone missing. I'd been about to sleep with him, my husband a room away.

Jean-Paul finally deigned to say one word, enunciated precisely,
delivered without an excess of feeling: "Asshole."

How could I tell Jean-Paul that Richie was the smell, the taste of
my childhood? It wasn't something you told your husband, it was
something you swallowed, and once it was down your gullet you
could keep other secrets, too. How could I tell Jean-Paul that all I
dreamed of, for weeks before we married, was Richie Daccapo?

One dinnertime the Daccapos got a knock on the door from an
LIRR man. From the Feeney house we heard Richie's sisters
scream out *No no, it's not true, it's not true.* Even my mother,
accustomed to high opera next door, was alarmed. She peered
through all the windows trying to see what was going on. I stood
behind her and watched Richie tear out the back door and make
his way across the yard to the grill, the altar, the holy site. I

thought he was going to put one hand on the cover, the way his father did, but instead he hammered it with his left fist. His pitching arm. I didn't once think about what I was about to do. I tore out of my own house, down the stairs, out the back door, through the rhododendrons. I hugged Richie from behind, hugged him with all the breath in my body. I knew it was his father, I knew his father was a goner, I'd known it all along. How could he not have a heart attack, running after Richie with a broom? For a while Richie kept punching the grill even with me hanging on his back, but I could feel him slowing down because I was there, because I wrapped my arms tighter and tighter around his waist. After a while he stopped and shook me off. "Why'd he make all those jokes about colored people, why'd he have to do that?"

"I know. My mother hates Italians even."

He went back in the house without another word, and I went back next door, and after a while you could hear them all settling down. "I'm sorry he walked away from you like that, Joan." My mother had watched everything.

"Good grief," my father said. "His old man's dead. Is he supposed to stop and chat?"

"I know you haven't been the best of friends with Richie lately," my mother said, ignoring my father as usual. "I know the family's coarse."

But when we walked into the wake Richie rose to comfort me, as if I were the mourner, and hugged me frontways, the proper way, the way we used to hug when we were small. And that was that, we were back, flesh against salty flesh, forever and always, fourteen and fifteen and sixteen, grieving Richie Daccapo the man of the house, his mother and his sisters driving him out of his frigging mind, but me, Joan Feeney, right next door, ready to snuggle and cuddle and smooch. Whatever we did, we wouldn't turn into our parents.

The night of our graduation, Richie told me I was crazy to go to the college both our fathers struggled through, night after exhausted night, a *Jesuit* school. *You ought to get out, man, get real, get away from the frigging priests. Come to Madison, we'll bust the place open.*

I'd been seeing him for months without his seeing me so maybe it shouldn't have surprised me that Richie had to get right up in my face while I was eyeballing paperbacks in the window of Community Books. "Feeney, I don't believe it. What are you doing in Brooklyn?"

"I live here." It was so anticlimactic: a Yankees cap on a Saturday afternoon. He looked ten years younger than I did—tanned, oiled, massaged—and his hug was gym-toned.

"Hey, so do I. Got myself a sweet brownstone in a recession sale." His Long Island accent, I noticed, had been diluted. The neighborhood where all the failures and the lefties came, thirty years ago, was full of guys who could afford Armani now. Richie got handsome when he got old, even surer of himself, if that was possible. I was a wreck—my straw hair was woven with gray, and I wasn't skinny anymore—but he leaned against the plate glass with all the time in the world. "It is so good to see you," he said, and I sucked up every syllable.

"What do I call you now?"

"You can call me Richie. You're the only one I'd let get away with it."

"No, I mean...you didn't change your name?" He looked at me as if I'd lost my wits. "When you went underground?"

He leaned his head back against the glass—you could hear a little *clunk*—and howled. "Oh my God."

"You didn't go underground?"

He wiped his eyes with the same fist that once slammed into his father's gas grill. "I played at going underground for about three weeks, and then I hightailed it back to Madison in time for finals. I was living in this neighborhood, actually, those three weeks. '72? '73?"

"'71. Weren't they looking for you, wasn't there a warrant?"

He shook his head. "Two of my, uhm, buddies got nabbed in a stolen car. That was a nasty business, I regret that. My prints were all over everything. I was convinced they were looking for me..."

He saw the look on my face and lowered his voice: "My friends had plastique." I'm not sure exactly why I didn't believe him, but my heart swooped the same way it used to when I saw him sidling up to other girls. Plastique was supposed to evoke Euro-terror: Baader-Meinhof and the IRA. Richie wanted to paint a hyperromantic picture—as if I needed help with *that*.

"But you made it back for finals."

"And into law school without a black mark to my name. Hey, what about you? What are you doing with yourself?"

No underground? No arrest warrant? *Law* school? One day he was fooling around with lightweight explosives, and the next day he was studying torts? "I teach."

"Acting?"

I realized then that I was ashamed, that I hadn't finished the sentence because I didn't want the well-dressed attorney to know what I did. "Middle school. You know, I thought maybe I saw you one morning on the D train."

"I wish I'd known, I would have bought you a cup of coffee. I can't tell you how many times I've told the sleepwalking story. Maybe I could buy you that coffee right now."

"Oh, I'm sorry," I said, though I had time to kill, my children long gone and Jean-Paul off at the restaurant. Immediately I regretted turning him down—who was being the snob? "Why don't you come over for a meal? Come over tonight. Bring your family."

He did a little Springsteen swivel. "No wife at the moment," he said, "and the girlfriend's traveling. Might be a good night for catching up, huh?"

When I called Jean-Paul on his cell, to tell him Richie Daccapo was coming to dinner, he said: "Who's Richie Daccapo?" But he remembered well enough when Richie showed up at the front door, or maybe he remembered how Richie affected me. The two of them started pawing the ground over drinks—too many drinks—and the three of us staggered through the apartment to the dinner table.

I was shocked at my middle-aged heart, thunkathunking over this guy I used to love. Jean-Paul doused him with questions, and Richie gave a lawyer's cautious answers: he'd been divorced for ten years now, his girlfriend was in Singapore, closing a deal. Jean-Paul wouldn't let up. Big firm? Been there long? Richie rolled his eyes, calculated: "Let's see . . . I made partner in '83." I blanched. For twenty years I'd been seeing him on a fishing trawler.

"You're a litigator?"

"Mergers and acquisitions. I live and die by the numbers."

Richie flashed an ironic smile in my direction, to remind me that I might have turned the corner on fifty but I was still a teenage girl.

Jean-Paul had thrown together the food, though he rarely cooked at home: he was a chef now, in his father's restaurant. We were working our way through avocado and endive, or at least Jean-Paul and I were. Richie had swallowed his salad down in two bites, as if to show how puny it was. He was giving Jean-Paul as good a third degree as he got: Where was the restaurant? How many reviews? How many stars?

Jean-Paul spluttered at *stars*. Pascal was a little café on the edge of Hell's Kitchen. Actors went there. "I'm not usually home Saturday night. Joan insisted."

Richie gave me a wink to suggest I should have insisted the opposite. "Whatever happened to the acting biz?"

"We were bad actors," I said. "Anyway, I was. Jean-Paul did—"

"Commercials, voiceovers." He left it at that, left out how he went to Madison Avenue in the eighties and got laid off just after we bought the apartment, left out that going back to his father was the hardest thing he'd ever done. We had three children by then. He sized Richie up again, from his end of the table—he'd sat him down at the opposite end, so they could stare at each other properly. "You have kids?"

"My partner makes maternal noises from time to time, but I'm not sure I could bring any more kids into the world after 9/11."

That shut us all up. We didn't do the *where were you* thing—we'd done it once too often. I'd never once dreamed that Richie Daccapo might be downtown in a white-shoe law firm.

Finally I said: "Our oldest, Paul—he's in law school, you might appreciate this—got busted down in Washington, protesting the war. His dean really made him sweat it."

"I guess he won't make that mistake again," Richie said.

Jean-Paul said: "What mistake?"

"Mistakes of our youth." Richie gave me another almost-wink, but Jean-Paul was not amused. He got hot at the dinner table, even without Richie Daccapo sitting down at the other end. His family always chewed up religion and politics with their meals, the subjects forbidden in the Feeney household, and sometimes I thought that was why I married him. He cracked our windshield with his fist when he heard on the car radio that Reagan had fired the air traffic controllers. Our kids called him the Last Socialist: he was the guy who stayed up all night e-mailing urgent appeals for prisoners on death row. Now the Last Socialist calculated if he could take the Corporate Lawyer. "You think it was a mistake, protesting Vietnam?"

Richie raised his glass. "Here's to the sixties. Here's to those protests."

"But not to these protests?" Jean-Paul had just about worn himself out over this war. He'd been to every march, got penned in on Second Avenue, had a mounted cop rear up on him—just like the old days.

Richie flashed a rueful smile. "These are different days. A kid in law school's got to be careful."

"I can't believe it. After the kind of trouble you—"

Richie scraped his chair around, ducked his head in a way that was supposed to be modest and charming. "I was full of myself."

"Well, our son's not full of himself."

"That's not what I meant."

"What did you mean, exactly?" You could almost hear the two of them growling. They'd stopped turning my way with winks and nods. They were only bearing down on each other. I was invisible: the middle-aged woman, the middle-school teacher, the monkey in the middle.

Richie pretended he was searching for the right words. "Anybody who plans to take the bar has to be cautious these days. After 9/11..."

"After 9/11, maybe he feels the urgency."

"Ah, youth. I remember..."

"What do you remember? Being *on the lam*?"

"Well, what do you remember? *Letters to the editor*?"

"After 9/11," Jean-Paul said, and now you could see that his heart was the one thunkathunking, "it's a pity to raise the body count."

"My, you are the unrepentant liberal, aren't you?"

It might have been the way he said *my*, the way he made Jean-Paul sound so quaint and old-fashioned and womanish. Or maybe it was the *liberal*. Jean-Paul took his time, inhaled a deep actorly breath. "I said back then that you jerks would be working for the Bank of America."

Richie said: "I don't work for the Bank of America. I'm with Feckersham Wiltonberry Raft." It was supposed to be a joke, I think.

"It was all just a rush for you, wasn't it? Making like you were out to save the world when you only wanted a cheap thrill."

Richie snorted. "*Cheap Thrills* is a classic, and Joplin's a saint. Otherwise, I don't know what you're talking about."

"You know exactly what I'm talking about. What's a few innocent bystanders when this building blows? What's a few hundred workers laid off in this merger? What's a few Iraqi kids under this bomb?" Jean-Paul had delivered his share of wine-induced diatribes over the years, but he'd never been quite so sweeping. He rose, to make the pronouncement official. "I'll have to ask you to leave. I don't want any neocons sitting at my table."

"Hey, now, did you hear me say I was a neocon? I'll have to ask *you* to stick to the facts as you know them."

"The fact is, you were willing to get us all busted right along with you. And now you criticize our son, who's out there putting his ass on the line."

"I don't like your tone." When Richie rose from his own chair the room got still, but I could hear the little crackle you hear just before the light bulb explodes. I watched Jean-Paul hoist up his end of the table, watched the restaurant crockery and glasses go sliding down toward Richie. The hollandaise drooled onto his Saturday night black jeans: the only piece of clothing on him that Springsteen might have worn. Richie picked up the plate with the last clinging avocado slice and flung it back the length of the table, where Jean-Paul ducked precisely in the nick of time. His stage training. He crouched beside the table, waiting for more lobs. "You were sleepwalking through Vietnam, too."

Richie found another shard to hurl, hesitated. You could see him consider heaving the little guy, pitching him through the window. Then you could see him calculate the cost. He released a slider and turned his back. "Not the best reunion, Feeney," he said. "Next time, my place."

Jean-Paul hurled a wineglass from down below, but it didn't get close. "Not going to be a next time, asshole." Richie was already halfway to the door, and then we heard the latch click.

"Well," I said. "I'm glad you got that out of your system."

My husband rose painfully on his bad knees and beat his Wild Man chest. "I should have kicked him out thirty years ago, before he kept me up the whole damn night."

"I'm sorry, Jean-Paul." Meaning, I think, sorry about that night, about this night, about all the disappointment and bitterness we had accumulated through the years. Maybe I was sorry I was a middle-aged woman who still saw herself squeezed between two twenty-year-old boys.

"Well, I'm not sorry." He scooped everything into the tablecloth, the way they would have done at Pascal. He was exhilarated. "I've got a long list of people I'd like to throw a few dishes at. All those loudmouths who used to be leftier than thou. Why don't you invite Paul Berman to dinner? David Horowitz?"

An hour later he was still pumped, full of adrenaline, ready to take off. From bed, twisting in the sheets, I watched him at his e-mail. We ran a two-shift marriage, one of us always asleep before the other, but a long marriage, too: a steady faithful family guy. It was a miracle that he lived to be older than my father got to be.

We had a bad stretch in the eighties. I sleepwalked through that time, literally: I wanted out of there, out of town. I went from bed to bed, touching my children's foreheads. The next morning they told me how they woke to see their mad mother staring down, tracing their faces. One or the other always walked me back to my own bed, back to my husband's side. Gracie, our middle child, caught me one night leaving the apartment. I was in my nightgown, but I'd thought to grab my wallet.

"Why you think he went right up to that cop?"

Jean-Paul didn't even stop typing. "Wanted to get caught." Not a second's hesitation. "Wanted somebody to stop him."

The way I went to my children's beds, so they would stop me.

But nobody stopped Richie. After his father died, his mother bought him a little Fiat convertible with the insurance money, and he raced it faster and faster down the Long Island Expressway. *Please, Richie, not so fast.* I never said it out loud: maybe I didn't want to go that fast, and maybe I did. *Please, you're gonna get us killed.* Ninety-seven, a hundred and two. *Somebody's gonna get hurt like this.* A hundred and five, one-ten. He was the coolest guy in high school, the alpha male, girls hanging off him: he even got elected vice president of the Afro-American Society, though he didn't actually go to the meetings. I picked the one who went to the meetings, the one who married me when my father was dying, the one who wrote the e-mails late into the night.

The third time he went sleepwalking that night, Richie knew better than to get near the pile of pots and pans. He crawled into our bed instead, the way he might have crawled in with his parents when he was small...or maybe he thought he was cavorting in some commune after all. When I woke at dawn he was pressed against one side of me, Jean-Paul against the other, their bodies rising with the sun: one heart racing, one heart murmuring, the heart in the middle ready to burst.

We were clinging to each other. We were kids on the run.

Instead Of

This is a story about *not* doing; this is a story about *everything else*. The trouble with writing is that it's too easy *not* to do. Imagine if eating chocolate was as easy *not to do* as writing. Or paying your mortgage. Or making an eight o'clock class. Imagine if you were firmly convinced that all the stupid things you do *instead of* writing were also more important than sex. Oh, no, I don't want to take you doggie-style, I have to check my e-mail.

The other day I counted. Sometimes I count things. I counted all the times I'd made love to my wife. It's not like I'm compulsive. It's not like I scratched a notch on the wall every time we did it. No. I took an average of the number of times a week and multiplied it by the number of weeks in the number of years we'd been together. Then I ran into my wife's office to tell her. "We have made love over 5,600 times."

Do you know that look you see on people's faces when they read the latest Darwin Awards, given to those who are honored posthumously for pathetic stupidity? Like the allergic beekeeper who invented a way to avoid fatal stings by sealing his head in a plastic bag? My wife looked genuinely astonished.

"It's true," I said. "I counted."

"Why in the world would you do that?" she asked.

Well, the true answer was, because I was writing. And I did this *instead*.

Over the course of thirty years, instead of sitting down at my desk every day to write, I went back to graduate school twice. I became an actor in summer stock. I began a publishing company. I had an affair with a woman who had a four-year-old child and I assumed all the responsibilities of fatherhood—while I was living with another woman. I developed a cocaine habit that cost the same as a Volvo S80 sedan with all-wheel drive and a sunroof. I ran for public office, and won, and found myself running a small municipal government.

This is Chapter One. This is the story of the first time. Gore

Vidal says that everyone born in America between 1895 and 1950 wanted to be a movie star. In an essay about F. Scott Fitzgerald and his wife, Zelda, Vidal says that *instead of* becoming movie stars, they decided to live like movie stars, based on movies that were complete fantasy. Zelda became a mental patient and Scott one of literature's most famous alcoholics. Before I wanted to be a writer I wanted to be a movie star, but *instead of* applying to drama school, or taking small roles in boring school plays, or going through the rounds of hundreds of humiliating auditions, I decided to be discovered.

There was a girl in my high school whose father was an important agent to television stars. Every year he took his daughter to the Emmy Awards ceremony in New York City, about thirty miles away from the old seaside resort town where I grew up in a red brick apartment building across the street from the boardwalk.

Somewhat overweight, shy, and often taken for a snob, Allison lived in the only house in my town with a swimming pool. She wore A-line skirts and cashmere sweater sets and had a miniature poodle named Brandy. With all his wealth and connection, her father seemed delighted that a boy was finally paying attention to his unpopular daughter, even a boy whose family lived five to a four-room apartment that always smelled of fried food from the boardwalk concessions. Allison's mother, too, seemed fond of me. A sun-wizened ex-Broadway chorus girl with a cigarette-raspy voice, she spent most of her time at the Club playing golf, and the rest in Manhattan, meeting her husband for drinks and dinner, leaving Allison to the care of a housekeeper who was suspicious of all male mammals that had not been gelded. Marina was a large, round Lithuanian woman who lived in a room in the basement. A kerchief always covering her head, she wore a crucifix the size of a Bowie knife, and had the hard round body of the outer mama in a set of Russian nesting dolls. Marina doted on Allison, whom she had effectively raised, and looked at me like a mouse turd on a white lace tablecloth. I could hardly explain to her that my feelings for Allison were completely pure. I merely wanted her father to make me a teenage television star.

Marina studied me while we ate tuna sandwiches for lunch, while we did homework together after school. If we were watching one of Allison's father's clients on television, Marina was crocheting on the couch; if we were in the sunroom, she was washing windows. Softly spoken, demurely dressed, Allison was in all ways modest in front of Marina, doubly so before her parents. Having never counted on sex in the first place, I set my sights on an introduction to the famous show people that kept her father on the telephone every night and, come summer, an invitation to the Emmy Awards ceremonies where he secured a large table for his clients and friends, Alan King, the comedian who appeared on the *Ed Sullivan Show;* and the great actor, Peter Ustinov; the singer Dinah Shore; and Soupy Sales, the target of my aspirations, who had teenage guests on his weekly show, and thereby started many careers. Every Sunday after Memorial Day, Allison's father prepared a barbecue for his less famous friends, retired B-movie actors and former Broadway dancers, no one I had remotely heard of, but who were openly gay and played suggestive games of charades and broke into Cole Porter songs at the piano. This was the life I was *supposed* to have been born to. With men in white pants who danced the mambo and bare-shouldered women who howled at their off-color jokes. I loved Allison's family and saw my future with them as the ladder to stardom, until one day an odd thing happened. Allison and I were in the pool. Her father was grilling porterhouse steaks and telling a story about the first time he met Sinatra—when I felt a hand in my bathing suit. It was Allison's hand, and it was no shy brush with temptation, but a determined attempt to milk the cow. Through the haze of Beefeater martinis and the rising smoke from the steaks, no one noticed.

Later that afternoon, when Allison and I were alone, I tried to kiss her, and got the cold shoulder in response. But the following week, during an episode of *Bonanza,* while Marina ducked into the laundry room to fold towels, I felt Allison's fingers gently tugging on my zipper. As Marina hummed a Lithuanian folk song, Allison stuffed her entire right hand inside my fly. Allison was turned on only at dangerous moments. Sometimes during sex, I dreamed aloud about being together in a motel room, all alone for a night, but on the rare occasion we found the house empty, Allison slapped my face if I made a move. I got my first blow job when her father ran upstairs to catch the last inning of a Yankees/Red Sox game. It may be that for the rest of my life I will associate cunnilingus with the sani-rinse cycle of the dishwasher because I spent many evenings on my knees between Allison's legs as she braced herself against the kitchen sink while Marina was walking the dog.

I was terrified of being found out, of being thrown out of the perfect family, but on Father's Day weekend her father himself asked if I'd like to be his daughter's date to the Emmy Awards ceremony, to sit at the head table with the family and all their famous friends. The idea of her oldest son within proximity of television stars awakened my mother's slumbering ambition to sing harmony with her two sisters in a nightclub act. She persuaded my father to rent me a tuxedo, while she prepared to remake me in the image of her favorite celebrity, an actor named George Hamilton, who had hair like Zorro and skin with the buffed polish of a goat-hide briefcase. As I more closely resembled Izak Perlman, a chubby young man with curly hair, it was to be a complicated makeover. But the stakes were high. I became the family project, and a three-fold plan was proposed. First, I needed a rich suntan. I also had to drop ten pounds, and my mom was going to straighten my hair.

Although the Sunday of the awards ceremony was a blazing ninety-four degrees, it came after a week of sporadic rain and unyielding humidity that spun my hair into a ball of steel wool. At sunrise I spread an old flannel blanket on the hot tar roof of my apartment building in an attempt to coax a fast suntan. In order to make up for lost time, my mother's kid brother Bobby, or The Idiot, as my father called him, also in on the project, provided me with a secret formula that he told me lifeguards used, a squeezer bottle with equal parts baby oil and iodine. Like a rotisserie chicken, I turned and basted myself every half hour. I did not eat breakfast or go downstairs for lunch as I was fasting to take off extra pounds, and I did not realize the effects of the secret formula until I saw my dad's expression when he came up to the roof to get me.

"The Idiot told you to do that?" he said. My face looked like two Mr. Potato Head eyes stuck in a red delicious apple. My mom led me directly to the bathroom, where I sat on the toilet seat while she massaged hair-straightening mixture into my scalp. Then she wrapped my head in aluminum foil and moved me to the living room to watch the ball game while my hair set. Mel Allen, the Yankees sportscaster, was swabbing his face with a handkerchief. The infield in the Bronx, he announced, had reached ninety-seven degrees. Allison and her mom were to pick me up in a limousine at five. It was now four-fifteen. My dad plucked lint off the tuxedo he rented. He had gotten a deal on the season's most fashionable style because it was a winter model, made of mohair. My skin was beginning to blister. The thought of wearing it brought to mind the Iron Maiden, an implement of torture used in the Spanish Inquisition which I had read about in *Ripley's Believe It or Not:* a coffin-size black box with spikes welded inside the door, designed to puncture the eyeballs and private parts of the victim as it closed. My mom unwrapped my head. "Oh, my," she said with the expression of someone unpinning a diaper. "It must be the heat." My hair looked like chocolate syrup on a volleyball.

My family accompanied me downstairs when the limousine arrived. Most of the children in the building had never seen a real chauffeur. An overly solicitous bodybuilder in an ill-fitting double-breasted suit, he held open the door and softly said many things about my comfort. It did not register at first that he was mumbling apologies, the air conditioning in the limo did not work. Allison was wearing a real ruby tiara and a shoulder-less pink satin gown that made crunching sounds as she slid over. Her mother was cursing the limousine company. I found that if I did not move, if I remained motionless and simply visualized a water moccasin sliding across my foot, that I could ignore the fact that my body was covered with second-degree burns. Relief arrived with a sea breeze as we swung through empty streets, and even Allison's mother had gently succumbed to sleep. But soon we hit the Long Island Expressway, packed bumper-to-bumper with Sunday beach traffic.

Enveloped in the exhaust of many thousands of cars headed back to Manhattan, the long black limousine did not move. Allison's mother snored. My slacks, ordered a size too small at the waist to account for the weight I was supposed to lose, girded the soft flesh of my belly like piano wire. To our right a car full of teenagers in bathing suits with their feet stuck out the window drank beer and smoked pot and, laughing at the limousine and the formally dressed people, took turns spitting phlegm loogies at us. Closing the windows was not an option. I tried blocking them out with a technique called Sylva Mind Control that I had read about in *Reader's Digest*. Concentrate. Soon the traffic would budge, soon we would pull up to the Americana Hotel on Broadway. A loogie hit me in the neck. Soon I would be on national television. Soon, I would eat. I had not eaten in twenty-four hours, and my stomach made those kinds of noises you hear in cars that need a new transmission. Lurching forward a car length at a time, swinging into lanes that abruptly stopped the moment we moved into them, we made slow progress.

The hand on my zipper came as a surprise, but Allison's expression was familiar, the one that always said, "Now, take me now. Now that Marina is carrying the garbage out; now that my parents are watching *The Waltons*, I want you now. Now that the chauffeur is blasting his horn at traffic, and my mother is two inches away, snoring, let's do it now," and Allison performed what is today known as a lap dance as we entered the Queens Midtown Tunnel.

The Americana Hotel was a gold brick and white marble anomaly on Seventh Avenue. The lobby was twenty-five stories high and walled with glass. A sidewalk with striped paving extended around the semicircular rotunda. We swung into a line of limousines. Allison's father, alarmed that we were over an hour late, pushed the chauffeur aside and ushered his wife and daughter from the back seat. This was my moment to shine. Born to a family of crude working people always in the midst of argument, I was entering a world of women in rhinestone ball gowns and witty men in black tuxedos. The air conditioning churned, cold as a Moscow Palace, and Dr. Zhivago was surrounded by admirers. It *was* Zhivago, Omar Sharif himself, with a bushy mustache and liquid chocolate eyes. Allison's father was making introductions. "Omar, I'd like you to meet my wife," he said, "and my daughter." Omar Sharif lowered his eyes and kissed Allison's wrist with a modest smile. "Meet my daughter's beau," he turned to the great actor Peter Ustinov. I shook his hand. I took a cocktail from a waiter's tray. "Meet Lorne Greene from *Bonanza*. Meet Andy Griffith."

Allison grabbed my elbow. "Are you all right?" she said. Lorne caught me under the arm. I seemed to have stumbled. I had never felt better in my entire life. The waiter offered more cocktails all around.

"Am I all right?" What a question. Instead of high-school lunch meat there were waiters in white carving *châteaubriand,* serving mounds of iced jumbo shrimp with silver tongs. I took another cocktail.

"You're drooling," Allison said.

"I am not drooling," I said. I was, however, quite violently shivering, and my skin was liquid slick. I was wet all over, but warm inside, the way you feel when you piss yourself in a wetsuit. There was a gelatinous ooze on my upper lip, but it was only perspiration, which I swabbed with a pink cocktail napkin.

"I want to introduce you to Garry Moore," her father said, taking Allison by the elbow to meet the famous variety show host with his signature bow tie and crewcut. I shook his hand, trying to ignore the sensations erupting in my belly, which now, many years later, I can best describe by recalling Sigourney Weaver's first contractions as the Alien swam circles in her abdomen. "Meet Durward Kirby," her father introduced me to the celebrated second banana.

I did perhaps need to sit down, but at the end of a reception line I spied Soupy Sales, the famous comedian and the evening's emcee, my ultimate goal. Instead of waiting on line to use the bathroom in my parents' crowded apartment, I'd be moving to Manhattan. Instead of greasy butchers and camera salesmen, I'd have book editors as neighbors, educated people in fascinating professions. I'd seen *Breakfast at Tiffany's* and knew I was suited to the Village, where on Sundays I'd wash my sheets in Laundromats with flight attendants. I'd eat in small ethnic restaurants where the owners would remember my favorites. My friends would be actors and naïve fledgling chorus girls from the Midwest. "Meet Soupy!" Allison's father said, but all I saw were the million glass beads of the ballroom chandeliers, spinning above me like the massive cones of giant crystal brassieres. I remember prisms of lamplight, silver, white, then a thousand shards of color, a kaleidoscope of famous faces, as I fell to one knee and pitched forward. Allison screamed. Soupy stepped away, shaking vomit from his shoe. I retched again and fell face forward.

Instead of a seat at the round table for twelve in front of the orchestra, I awoke on a king mattress with a striped duvet whose pattern matched the wallpaper, in a suite on the eighteenth floor. It was in fact Soupy's suite. "Make sure the asshole is out of there before I get upstairs," I heard him say as two waiters carried me to the elevator. He was very witty tonight. He was the host. I watched on TV as Allison sat at the edge of the bed. There was a bottle of Pepto-Bismol on the night table. And an ice bucket with a wash towel draped over the side. My shoes were off, as were my tight pants and the itchy wool jacket. I was feeling much, much better.

I was under no illusion. I had blown my chances. Instead of an easy entrée to stardom, it was back to my senior year of high school. I had ruined any possibility to be discovered. I was now a family footnote. The subject of a poolside reminiscence as the steaks sizzled and the martinis were poured. Instead of an acting job in Manhattan I was facing state college and a work-study job.

The orchestra cued the emcee. The camera panned the ballroom. Allison was sitting cross-legged, her chin in her palms, as the blue TV glare shimmered on her bare shoulders.

Soupy told a joke. Fifty tables roared approval. I inched up to the front of the bed and sat next to her. At the commercial break I said, "I am sorry," and lay my head against her arm.

"I embarrassed you and your family," I said. "I tried too hard." Without taking her eyes from the screen, she put her palm to my forehead. We watched another segment in silence. Florence Henderson took the award for Best Actress in a weekly comedy series.

"Do you realize we've never been alone before?" I said. "No Marina. No parents hovering around."

To this point I had never seen her naked, never seen more than snatches of her body in the shadows. "But here we are with a huge bed and hours of time alone."

Allison sighed as I touched my tongue to her earlobe, turned swiftly, and caught me square in the face with the knuckles of her closed fist.

Instead of returning to my apartment building with the promise of a future in show business, I was helped from the limousine holding a wet washcloth to a very black eye.

ABOUT MARTÍN ESPADA

A Profile by César A. Salgado

When Martín Espada turned twenty, a family friend gave him a copy of the anthology *Latin American Revolutionary Poetry*. Along with the gift, the friend ventured some words of prophecy: *"Tú también serás poeta,"* he told Espada—"You will also become a poet." The book had been edited by Roberto Márquez, a Nuyorican (New York–born Puerto Rican) professor of working-class roots. It collected translations of political poems by Latin American authors whose radicalism had been newly galvanized in the wake of Pinochet's U.S.-supported coup of Allende's socialist government in Chile.

Espada had previously toyed with the idea of becoming a writer when he'd attended the University of Maryland for one year. He dropped out after one professor reprimanded him for admiring Allen Ginsberg and another chided his work as "too hostile." Even so, the poems in Márquez's book had a deep, transforming impact on Espada. They revealed a rich literary heritage, one from which he did not, for once, feel excluded. "I was thunderstruck," he recalls. "I was no longer a poetic amnesiac. All of a sudden I found a tradition to identify with, I found a place where I could sit... You think you are standing on the street all by yourself with a picket sign and then you hear a noise and you turn around and you see a demonstration four blocks long." The image of the picket line as a sudden, uplifting apparition reflects some key values in Espada's poetry: building communal solidarity as a way to confront social alienation and exploitation, maintaining an unwavering political commitment against great odds, and perceiving *designios* (prophetic signs) in everyday circumstances.

Raised in the blighted East New York section of Brooklyn as the son of a Puerto Rican community organizer, Martín Espada began participating in political demonstrations at a young age; they were the subjects of his earliest childhood drawings. Upon discovering the deep social concerns in the writings of Pablo Neruda, Nicolás Guillén, Ernesto Cardenal, Pedro Pietri, and others featured in Márquez's book, Espada saw the picket line he had drawn as a child morph suddenly into an international chorus of activist poets from a never-dying Hispanic tradition. Nurtured by this legacy, Espada went back to college in Madison, Wisconsin. He eked out money for tuition and rent by working in a bar, a ballpark, a gas station, a primate lab, and a transient hotel. He majored in History, focusing on Latin America, and traveled to Nicaragua to witness the Sandinista Revolution up close. Then he got a law degree at Northeastern University in Boston and represented Spanish-speaking immigrants as a tenant lawyer in Chelsea, Massachusetts, until 1993. He wrote poetry throughout these years: "I started writing again and never looked back."

Before leaving Madison for Boston, Espada published *The Immigrant Iceboy's Bolero* (1982). The book's mixing of assertive urban poems with striking photos of dilapidated barrio life (taken by Espada's father) paid homage to the anthology *Nuyorican Poetry,* which had established the Nuyorican socio-aesthetic agenda. Following these poets' lead, the work in Espada's first book documents the institutional neglect suffered by Latinos in rundown inner cities and crop fields. Each poem is also a paean to the persistence and dignity with which immigrants survive abuse and uncertainty: "fishermen wading into the North American gloom" who could pull out "a fierce gasping life / from the polluted current."

The Boston scene boosted Espada's career as a poet in unexpected ways. While working as a legal intern at the Migrant Legal Action Program, Espada applied for a writing fellowship, sending some poems on a whim; he received $5,000, for once making "more money as a poet than as a legal worker." Espada thus became a regular presence at poetry readings in Boston's community centers and university campuses, finding enough breathing room to finish his second book, *Trumpets from the Islands of Their Eviction* (1987), shortly after earning his law degree. Here he puts forth what he has called his "poetry of advocacy," zeroing in on the many legal subterfuges that complicate and worsen the immigrant's plight in North America. The poet-now-lawyer moves from the streets into the courtroom, where he unveils the mistreatment of minorities throughout U.S. legal history. The eviction in the title not only names the state-enforced homelessness

Katherine Gilbert-Espada

that afflicts many immigrants; it is Espada's metaphor for the colonial underpinnings of diaspora itself, of the displacements that expanding empires force upon the populations they occupy after supplanting their native system of rights.

In his third book, *Rebellion Is the Circle of a Lover's Hands* (1990), winner of the Paterson Poetry Prize and the PEN/Revson Fellowship, Espada takes leave of many idiosyncrasies in Nuyorican poetry to engage in methodical historical reflection and cement himself in his own style and trade. He avoids compulsive "Spanglish" wordplay and composes a rigorous bilingual collection; the poems in English on the left page are rendered meticulously into Spanish on the right. An intricate and calculated verse construction sets Espada's work apart from the spontaneous gestural and oral inflections, the slang and swagger, that are the trademarks of the Nuyorican street poet's performance. Espada's disregard for the improvisational qualities in Nuyorican poetry comes from his commitment to fashion through his poems a type of "verbal monument" that can bear witness to Puerto Rico's and other Latino nations' struggle under U.S. neocolonial hegemony.

Espada's reputation has been on a meteoric rise ever since. In 1990, Earl Shorris predicted in *The New York Times* that Martín

Espada would become "*the* Latino poet of his generation." In a 2002 blurb, Sandra Cisneros thought of him as a potential U.S. Poet Laureate, calling him "the Pablo Neruda of North American authors." Controversy has only helped increase his stature. When National Public Radio commissioned Espada to create a poem inspired by current news events, he wrote about the plight of Mumia Abu-Jamal, on death row for a hotly disputed murder conviction. Apparently, the network thought the poem's polemical topic would compromise government or private funding and chose not to air it; many rallied to Espada's side when he interpreted the network's decision as a form of censorship. He also made headlines when he turned down Nike's offer to write a poem for an Olympic advertising campaign in a public letter, rebuking Nike's brutal, exploitative labor practices in Asia. Few poets, Latino or mainstream, have raised the temperature of political and literary debate with such visibility and topicality.

Although well-deserved, all this attention is somewhat ironic, as it recognizes the expression of a poet who, following Neruda, often hushes his own voice so that those of the long-silenced and marginalized can be heard through his poems. It gives center stage to someone whose visionary breadth brings to mind Walt Whitman's ebullient American outlook, yet identifies strongly with the periphery of "minority" and "Third World" subjects and sharply criticizes the multicultural deficits of the current academic canon. It seeks U.S. Poet Laureate status for a writer who captures the changing rhythms of the American vernacular as ably and scrupulously as William Carlos Williams, yet remains stubbornly Puerto Rican, another *independentista* in the island's forceful lineage of politically minded, anti-colonial poets such as Clemente Soto Vélez and Juan Antonio Corretjer, and Caribbean cadence-masters such as Luis Palés Matos.

That Espada's work stands at the crossroads of many non-literary fields and concerns—law, ethnicity, colonialism, history, public memory, urban and diaspora studies, language politics—is proof of how poetry can become more politically efficacious with superior craft; the better its aesthetic and cognitive makeup, the greater its potential social relevance and impact. The new poems in Espada's latest book, *Alabanza*, which means praise, are a case in point. Each piece is a carefully engineered capsule of political epiphany in which a richly suggestive, often elaborate, riddle-like title helps the reader navigate the symbolic dimensions of a concrete social story.

In 1993, Espada's wish to be part of an English university program finally came to fruition. His literary accomplishments helped him secure a faculty position in English at the University of Massachusetts, Amherst, where he now teaches creative writing workshops and seminars on the life and works of Pablo Neruda and on Latino poetry. Full-time employment as a professor has let him branch out into new literary endeavors as an anthologist and essayist. For Curbstone Press, he edited a collection of works by the publisher's political poets, *Poetry Like Bread* (1994). For the University of Massachusetts Press, he put together *El Coro* (1997), a compilation of recent Latino and Latina poetry, which received the Gustavo Myers Outstanding Book Award. His collection of essays, *Zapata's Disciple* (1990), published by South End Press, won the Independent Publisher Book Award.

In the last fifteen years, Espada has kept a busy schedule of readings nationwide that has earned him a visibility unequaled among Latino poets. He has also increased the rhythm of his poetic output and expanded the range of his themes and concerns. Since joining the faculty of the University of Massachusetts, he has published three new poetry collections with W.W. Norton: *City of Coughing and Dead Radiators* (1993), *Imagine the Angels of Bread* (1996), and *A Mayan Astronomer in Hell's Kitchen* (2000). *Imagine* won an American Book Award and was a finalist for the National Book Critics' Circle Award. In 2003, Norton published a comprehensive anthology of Espada's work, *Alabanza: New and Selected Poems 1982–2002*, an American Library Association Notable Book of the Year and the recipient of the Paterson Award for Sustained Achievement. The book ends with a postscript of seventeen new poems written in 2002 in the light of significant personal and national events: a first trip to Ireland, health problems in his family, and the anniversary of the 9/11 Twin Towers attack.

The poems explore new directions that broaden even more the geopolitical horizons within Espada's poetic reach. The Chelsea courtroom, the Brooklyn projects, the Puerto Rican cemetery, and the New England woods no longer act as the main setting for a poem, but as one among many wider frames of reference that

go well beyond Neruda's own New World hemispheric bound-
aries. *Alabanza* coalesces a new array of ethnoscapes—an Old San
Juan street during a strongly Africanized San Sebastián festival;
the pastoral yet history-scarred Irish scenery of Achill Island; the
Mexican metropolis, heartland, and borderland; the Arab
World—to fashion poems that celebrate the overlapping of
immigrant, revolutionary, and anti-colonial experience across
American and non-American nations. The Puerto Rican
cordillera is evoked in an Irish mountain range; blacklisting in
post-Zapatista Mexico recalls repression in 1973 post-Allende
Chile; Carl Sandburg's bookish shyness as a young Illinois army
recruit in the 1898 Spanish-American War is juxtaposed with
great-grand-uncle Luis Espada's thespian antics as a colorful cigar
factory reader and literature lover; bombed Afghan refugees and
Manhattan Latinos address each other in "constellations of
smoke." The poems behave no longer as straightforward anec-
dotes but as novelistic fields of interlocking transnational stories,
with lengthier stanzas and verses and a weightier presence of the
poet's persona acting as side character, as narrator, as singer, as
prophetic seer.

Following the cosmic propensities in Neruda, Soto Vélez, and
Corretjer's celebration of the working poor, Espada shows us that
poetry exercised as praise for the exploited and the ignored helps
us realize the multidirectional interconnectedness of all human
experience in space and time. Through such homage, we recognize how the disenfranchised are those who weave the innermost
fabric of history.

*César A. Salgado is Associate Professor in the Department of Spanish and
Portuguese and the Program in Comparative Literature at the University of
Texas at Austin. He is the author of* From Modernism to Neobaroque: Joyce
and Lezama Lima *(2001). The profile above draws from previous articles on
Espada published by the author.*

*Books Recommended by
Our Staff Editors*

Wedding Day, *poems by Dana Levin* (Copper Canyon): Intimate and hypnotic, the poems of Levin's wonderful second book operate as a lens through which we are simultaneously granted two views: one into the darker, private interior of the self, the other of an outer-world turned otherworldly by the poet's eye. Whether turning her gaze inward or outward, these poems question the moral, aesthetic, and metaphysic needs that poetry exists to fulfill; Levin posits a lovely and revelatory analogy when she likens the "American poet" to "[a] cricket trilling endlessly against the din of traffic. / Inaudible, unless you stood right at the spot where it lodged itself in a little crack between the walk and the wall . . . legg[ing] the air ceaselessly where no one could hear it." —*Cate Marvin*

Nice Big American Baby, *stories by Judy Budnitz* (Knopf): The breadth of these stories, from Kafkaesque surrealism to tightly wrought naturalism, is breathtaking in itself, but what unites this extraordinary collection is its unnerving verve and vision. There isn't anything Judy Budnitz can't or won't do, and right when you think she couldn't possibly be more inventive and daring and smart and universal, she proves you wrong. Almost every story both surpasses and defeats the reader's expectations, from a tale about an immigrant baby four years in vitro to one about a Russian mail-order bride who transcends and undermines the American society that adopts her. "Near-death experience?" the unhappy wife asks. "I

have been having one of these for years. I am having it right now." This collection is a joyful book, one that knows the difference between sharp social commentary and captivating narrative, and gets both right. —*Fred Leebron*

The Return Message, *poems by Tessa Rumsey* (Norton): The foremost organizing principal of this fascinating second volume is the manner in which Rumsey pairs poems beneath shared titles and erects a dialogue between the shorter, pastoral poems that occupy the left pages and the longer, cityscape poems on the right. The dense scent of wisteria spills over into a metallic, mesmerizing city-of-self the speaker has erected: "We were in collusion, this city and I, creating a mythology of desolation . . ." Encoded in the complex and lush weave of language that characterizes these poems is a narrative of despair, loss, obsession, and paradoxical blossoming: "*To lead you,* said the clock, said the lover, *we must leave you.*" —*Cate Marvin*

The Train to Lo Wu, *stories by Jess Row* (Dial): In Jess Row's post-colonial Hong Kong, everything seems to be on the verge of disappearing. The city is a "mirage" that can be "swallowed in fog for days," the language slippery, "no tenses or articles, with seven different ways of saying the same syllable." No one can quite understand or apprehend each other in this debut collection. A young girl blindfolds herself to be sentient to her dead mother; a photographer decamps to a monastery to mull over his failing marriage; an American graduate student tries to manipulate a masseur into revealing his memories of the Cultural Revolution: "This is your problem," he tells her. "You only look with your eyes." Blindness and ghosts are frequent allusions—fitting, since *gwailo*, the word for *foreigner*, can also mean *ghost* or *demon*. But, as one expat says, the designation ultimately implies that they don't matter to the locals, they don't exist. In these seven quiet, deftly drawn stories, characters crisscross various demarcations of politics, history, race, and religion, but, agonizingly, they never seem able to locate one another, let alone themselves. —*Don Lee*

EDITORS' SHELF

Books Recommended by
Our Advisory Editors

Robert Boswell recommends *In the Shadows of the Sun,* a novel by Alex Parsons: "This is a startlingly good novel. Set during World War II in rural New Mexico and the jungles of the Philippines, *In the Shadows of the Sun* is not a war story but a story of familial tragedy. One could argue that it is ultimately about the tragedy of having faith in institutions. But this says little about the experience of reading the book, which is completely involving and finally transformative. This is Parsons's second novel, and there can't be any question about his gifts. He's a hugely talented writer and unlike anyone else of his generation." (Talese/Doubleday)

Donald Hall recommends *A Word Like Fire,* selected poems by Dick Barnes: "Barnes, who died five years ago, was little known in the East, but he was a man of vast energy. His knowledge was superb, and his talents went everywhere. He taught literature at Pomona College, performed with his own jazz band, wrote and staged enormous pup-

pet plays with fireworks, and translated Borges with Robert Mezey, who edited these poems posthumously. Plain language about the Western scene makes the best lines of these poems. They are original not just because of what they look at. He details the natural world, and the world of animals. He is a poet of mysterious matters of the spirit. He is a poet of humor, and his ears are as open as his eyes." (Handsel)

Donald Hall recommends *Playland: Poems 1994–2004,* by Eve Packer: "Eve was my student at Michigan, and much later my friend when I lived for a while in New York. It's one of those books about which people say, 'I couldn't put it down.' There is a liveliness and specificity about it, pure Manhattan, duly and boldly observed. They are not trying to be *Lycidas* (and there is nothing wrong with being *Lycidas*), but they are trying and doing something that modern American poetry occasionally does beautifully—the quick cut of American scenes, the words limited and exact, the poem and language perfectly fit to the moment. There are some Times Square bits that I like especially. By her poems, she is a photographer, and I salute her as the Weegee poet. Few of us have been able to write things so deft and accurate and modest and instant and exact and shocking." (Fly by Night)

Justin Kaplan recommends *The Peabody Sisters,* a biography by Megan Marshall: "A heroically researched and beautifully written biography about three women who were, in many ways, the American Brontës." (Houghton Mifflin)

Maxine Kumin recommends *Healed by Horses,* a memoir by Carole Fletcher with Lawrence Scanlon: "A remarkable story of a young woman burned over sixty-five percent of her body, who made it back through agonizing debridements and skin grafts to training and actually performing with her much-loved horses." (Atria)

Philip Levine recommends *Sky,* poems by Christopher Buckley: "Buckley is a California poet who—though he has published at least ten books—seems little known in the East. His poems are both Western and universal. It is the landscape of California that serves as the backdrop to the striving for significance that enriched his boyhood in Santa Barbara and was lost somewhere in that territory we call growing up. The poems are modest, straightforward, intensely lyrical, and totally accessible. Whether he is addressing his departed friend, the poet Ernesto Trejo, or the great swell of the Pacific Ocean that haunts his dreams, the voice is always the same, modest and direct. This is a humble poetry of great truths and profound emotions that never overstates its concerns for the events both in and above the world. It rewards countless readings and never betrays itself." (Sheep Meadow)

Chase Twichell recommends *Dark Under Kiganda Stars,* poems by Lilah Hegnauer: "This first book is a startling lyrical account of a young Catholic American student's time in Uganda, where she taught English in the Kiganda Highway Secondary School and assisted at a medical clinic in a remote country village. She was given several classes of students, a caning stick, and was told to 'teach anything.' Written while the author was still in college, it is an astonishing debut, richly musical

and descriptive, confident, unpretentious, and bursting with new experience: love, identity, religious faith, and the complex collisions of culture and language." (Ausable)

Ellen Bryant Voigt recommends *In the Blue Pharmacy,* essays by Marianne Boruch: "The same capacious mind on display in Boruch's selected poems is everywhere available here, as is her characteristic meditative structure, one that circles its subjects and their implications without any sort of didactic overreaching. In 'The Rage to Reorder,' the last piece in this new prose collection, she investigates a convincing alternative to the obsession with change over a poetic career, as in the 'breakthrough' narrative applied to Lowell and others, offering in its stead the increased 'range of motion' sought in muscular rehabilitation. Her exemplars are Elizabeth Bishop and the nest-building impulse of the English sparrow, but she might have used her own work as well (although such self-reference would no doubt be unthinkable to her), both her sly and nimble poems and these brilliant, evocative essays, a graceful record of a lifetime of deep, open, perceptive thinking about poetry and poems." (Trinity)

Dan Wakefield recommends *The Writing on the Wall,* a novel by Lynn Sharon Schwartz: "*The Writing on the Wall* is a novel that mines art and understanding out of the 9/11 nightmare, bringing the effects of the tragedy into individual lives of credible characters. The author's earlier masterwork, *Disturbances in the Field,* which follows the lives of three Barnard students into marriage, motherhood, and maturity, is being reissued this year." (Counterpoint)

New Books by
Our Advisory Editors

Mark Doty, *School of the Arts,* poems: Incisive and transcendent, Doty's seventh collection contemplates the creative process and eternal questions of love and loss, desire and despair. (HarperCollins)

Mary Gordon, *Pearl,* a novel: In Gordon's haunting new book, a woman re-examines her assumptions about politics and the church when she goes to Dublin to save her daughter, who is on a hunger strike. (Pantheon)

Marilyn Hacker, translation of *Birds and Bison,* poems by Claire Malroux: These are both urban and pastoral poems, marvelously observing the natural world, language, and the human spirit. (Sheep Meadow)

Alice Hoffman, *The Ice Queen,* a novel: In this enthralling tale, a small-town librarian is hit by lightning, and finds her heretofore frozen heart suddenly burning. (Little, Brown)

Maxine Kumin, *Jack and Other New Poems:* Kumin's powerful fourteenth collection contains her signature pastoral poems, but also meditations on the body, war, civil liberties, and the environment. (Norton)

Jay Neugeboren, *News from the New American Diaspora,* stories: The twelve stories in Neugeboren's illuminating new collection focus on Jews in various states of exile—strangers in strange lands, far from home. (Texas)

Howard Norman, *In Fond Remembrance of Me,* a memoir: A moving memoir of Norman's time in Manitoba, where he and an Anglo-Japanese woman—fatally ill, but an ardent spirit—were translating Inuit tales. (North Point)

Charles Simic, *My Noiseless Entourage,* poems: With his usual wry acuity, Simic explores love, futility, and the sense of an individual life in his fourteenth volume. (Harcourt)

Charles Simic, *Aunt Lettuce, I Want to Peek Under Your Skirt,* poems, with drawings by Howie Michaels: A playful salute to all things sexy in erotic poems and illustrations. (Tin House/Bloomsbury)

Gary Soto, *Help Wanted,* stories: A witty collection of ten young-adult stories about Latino youth in trouble, or looking for trouble, in the weirdness of everyday Fresno. (Harcourt)

Gerald Stern, *Everything Is Burning,* poems: Ruthless and occasionally outrageous, Stern's literary songs are sharp, surprising, and unerring in their delivery. (Norton)

CONTRIBUTORS' NOTES

Spring 2005

JACK AGÜEROS's books of poems include *Lord, Is This a Psalm?*, *Sonnets from the Puerto Rican,* and *Correspondence Between Stonehaulers.* He is also the translator of *Song of the Simple Truth: The Complete Poems of Julia de Burgos,* the author of *Dominoes & Other Stories from the Puerto Rican,* and a contributor to *Immigrant Experience: The Anguish of Becoming American.*

DOUG ANDERSON is at work on a memoir about the Vietnam War, the sixties, and recent friendships with Viet Cong who have become poets and fiction writers. His latest book of poems is *Blues for Unemployed Secret Police.* Current work has appeared in *Poetry* and *The Pushcart Prize XXIX.*

NIN ANDREWS is the author of several books, including *The Book of Orgasms* and *Why They Grow Wings.* Her newest collection, *Sleeping with Houdini,* is forthcoming from Tupelo in 2005.

NAOMI AYALA, a native of Puerto Rico, is the author of *Wild Animals on the Moon* (Curbstone, 1997). Her work has appeared in *Callaloo, The Village Voice, The Caribbean Writer, The Massachusetts Review, Hanging Loose,* and *Terra Incognita.* She is an M.F.A. student in the Bennington College Writing Seminars program.

MELISSA BANK won the Nelson Algren Award for short fiction in 1993. Her first book, *The Girls' Guide to Hunting and Fishing,* spent sixteen weeks on *The New York Times* bestseller list and was translated into twenty-eight languages. Her story in this issue will be included in her new book, *The Wonder Spot,* which will be published by Viking Penguin in June 2005.

QUANG BAO was born in Can Tho, Vietnam. His work has appeared in *The Threepenny Review, The New York Times,* and on NPR. He is the co-editor of *Take Out: Queer Writing from Asian Pacific America* and is the current executive director of The Asian American Writers' Workshop in New York City.

KAREN E. BENDER is the author of the novel *Like Normal People* (Houghton Mifflin). Her fiction has appeared in *The New Yorker, Granta, Zoetrope: All-Story, Story,* and other magazines. She teaches creative writing at the University of North Carolina at Wilmington.

DANIEL BERRIGAN is a Jesuit priest and peace activist who has been twice nominated for the Nobel Peace Prize. He has published over fifty volumes of poetry and prose, most recently *And the Risen Bread.* His first book of poems, *Time Without Number,* won the Lamont Poetry Prize, and his play *The Trial of the Catonsville Nine* won a Tony Award in 1972.

RICHARD BLANCO's *City of a Hundred Fires* received the 1997 Starrett Prize from the University of Pittsburgh Press. His work on the Cuban-American experience has appeared in numerous literary journals and anthologies. The poem in this issue is from his second book, *Directions to the Beach of the Dead*, forthcoming in 2005 from the University of Arizona Press.

MICHELLE BOISSEAU's third book of poetry, *Trembling Air* (Arkansas), appeared in 2003, as did the sixth edition of her text *Writing Poems*. She is Professor of English at the University of Missouri–Kansas City, where she is also associate editor of BkMk Press.

KEVIN BOWEN is director of the William Joiner Center for the Study of War and Social Consequences at the University of Massachusetts, Boston. His most recent collections are *Eight True Maps of the West* (Dedalus Press, Dublin) and, with Nguyen Ba Chung, *Six Vietnamese Poets* (Curbstone).

RAFAEL CAMPO teaches and practices internal medicine at Harvard Medical School and Beth Israel Deaconess Medical Center in Boston. His most recent books include *Diva* (Duke, 2000), a finalist for the NBCC Award in poetry; *Landscape with Human Figure* (Duke, 2002), winner of the Gold Medal from *ForeWord;* and *The Healing Art,* (Norton, 2003), essays on poetry and healing.

MARIA MAGDALENA CAMPOS-PONS was born and raised in Cuba, and trained at the Superior Institute of Art (ISA) in Havana. She has lived and worked in the Boston area since arriving in the U.S. in 1991, and has exhibited widely in this country and around the world. With Neil Leonard, she is the owner and founder of the Gallery Artists Studio Projects (GASP) in Brookline, Massachusetts.

CYRUS CASSELLS is the author of four books of poetry, *The Mud Actor, Soul Make a Path Through Shouting, Beautiful Signor,* and *More than Peace and Cypresses.* He is the recipient of a Lannan Literary Award and a Lambda Literary Award.

NAN COHEN's first book is *Rope Bridge* (Cherry Grove, 2005). A 2003 NEA fellow and a past Wallace Stegner Fellow and Jones Lecturer at Stanford, she lives in Los Angeles and is the poetry director of the Napa Valley Writers' Conference.

ROBERT CORDING teaches English and creative writing at the College of the Holy Cross. He has published four collections of poems: *Life-list,* which won the Ohio State University Press/*The Journal* Award in 1987; *What Binds Us to This World* (Copper Beech); *Heavy Grace* (Alice James); and *Against Consolation* (CavanKerry).

ROBERT CREELEY teaches in Brown's Graduate Program in Literary Arts. His most recent book is *If I Were Writing This* (New Directions).

THEODORE DEPPE is the author of four collections of poems, including *The Wanderer King* (Alice James, 1996) and *Cape Clear: New and Selected Poems* (Salmon Books, Ireland, 2002). His poems are included in recent issues of *The Southern Review, Sou'wester, Iron Horse Literary Review, Tar River Poetry,* and *Green Mountains Review.*

RICHARD GARCIA is the author of *Rancho Notorious* (BOA Editions). His poems have recently appeared in the web publications *Perihelion, The Blue Moon*

Review, The Cortland Review, and in the print journals *Sentence* and *Pool.* His next volume of poetry, *The Persistence of Objects,* is forthcoming from BOA Editions in 2006. His website is www.richardgarcia.info.

STEPHEN GIBSON is author of a poetry collection, *Rorschach Art* (Red Hen, 2001), as well as the story collection *The Persistence of Memory,* a finalist for the Flannery O'Connor Award and the Spokane Prize. New work can be found in *Epoch, McSweeney's Internet Tendency* and in The People's Press anthology *Familiar.* His poem here is from a new collection, *Masaccio's Expulsion.*

ARACELIS GIRMAY writes poetry, fiction, and essays. A Cave Canem fellow, she currently resides in her native California, where she leads community writing workshops. Her collage-based picture book, *Changing, Changing,* is forthcoming from George Braziller Publishers in spring 2005.

EUGENE GLORIA's first collection of poems, *Drivers at the Short-Time Motel,* a National Poetry Series selection, was published by Penguin Books. He has received the Asian American Literary Award and a Pushcart Prize, and his poems have appeared in *Prairie Schooner, The Gettysburg Review,* and elsewhere. He teaches English and creative writing at DePauw University.

ALYSON HAGY is the author of four works of fiction, including the story collection *Graveyard of the Atlantic* and the novel *Keeneland.* She lives and teaches in Laramie, Wyoming.

DONALD HALL will publish *The Best Day the Worst Day,* a memoir of his life with Jane Kenyon, in the spring of 2005. His most recent book of poems is *The Painted Bed.* More recently, he has collected essays about poetry in *Breakfast Served Any Time All Day,* and short stories in *Willow Temple.*

SAM HAMILL was Editor of Copper Canyon Press from 1972–2004. He is the author of more than forty volumes of poetry, poetry-in-translation, and essays. His book of new and selected poems and translations, *Almost Paradise,* was recently published by Shambhala. He founded Poets Against the War in 2003.

NATHALIE HANDAL is a poet, playwright, and writer. Her latest poetry book, *The Lives of Rain,* was shortlisted for the Agnes Lynch Starrett Poetry Prize. She is Poetry Books Review Editor for *Sable* (UK) and Associate Artist for the production company The Kazbah Project. She teaches at Columbia University.

MYRONN HARDY is a graduate of the University of Michigan and Columbia University. He is the author of the book of poems *Approaching the Center.* He lives in New York City.

DAVID HERNANDEZ is the author of *A House Waiting for Music* (Tupelo, 2003). His poems have recently appeared in *TriQuarterly, The Iowa Review, Quarterly West, Epoch,* and *Agni.* He is married to the writer Lisa Glatt, and his website is at www.DavidAHernandez.com.

BOB HICOK's most recent book is *Insomnia Diary* (Pittsburgh, 2004). He teaches in the M.F.A. program at Virginia Tech.

AL HUDGINS was born and raised in Virginia and now makes his home in Basking Ridge, New Jersey. His work has appeared in *The Georgia Review, Confrontation,* and elsewhere, and for eight years he served on the administrative staff of the Bread Loaf Writers' Conference.

COLETTE INEZ has authored nine poetry collections, most recently *Spinoza Doesn't Come Here Anymore* from Melville House Books, and has won Guggenheim, Rockefeller, and two NEA fellowships. She is widely anthologized and teaches in Columbia University's Writing Program. Her forthcoming memoir, *The Secret of M. Dulong,* will be published in 2005 by the University of Wisconsin Press.

YUSEF KOMUNYAKAA's latest book is *Taboo.* He teaches at Princeton University.

MELISSA KWASNY is the author of one book of poetry, *The Archival Birds* (Bear Star, 2000), as well as the editor of *Toward the Open Field: Poets on the Art of Poetry* (Wesleyan, 2004). She is currently Hugo Visiting Writer at the University of Montana.

ADRIAN C. LOUIS has worked in the Minnesota State University system since 1999. His most recent book of poems is *Evil Corn* (Ellis, 2004).

JULIO MARZAN has published two books of poetry, *Translations Without Originals* and *Puerta de Tierra,* as well as *The Spanish American Roots of William Carlos Williams* (Texas). He has also translated *Selected Poems: Luis Palés Matos* (Arte Público). Poems have appeared in *Harper's, Parnassus, The Massachusetts Review, Tin House,* and *New Letters.*

JOSHUA MCKINNEY is the author of *Saunter* (Georgia) and *The Novice Mourner* (forthcoming from Bear Star Press). His work has appeared in such journals as *American Letters & Commentary, Boulevard, Colorado Review, Denver Quarterly, The Kenyon Review, Poetry International, Volt,* and many others. He is an associate professor of English at California State University, Sacramento.

DAVID MURA has written three books of poetry, *Angels for the Burning* (BOA Editions, 2004), *The Colors of Desire,* and *After We Lost Our Way.* His book of criticism, *Songs for Uncle Tom, Tonto & Mr. Moto: Poetry & Identity,* appears in the University of Michigan's Poets on Poetry series.

JOHN MURILLO is the 2002 and 2004 winner of the D.C. Commission on the Arts and Humanities' Larry Neal Award for Poetry. He is a Cave Canem fellow and former instructor with DCWritersCorps.

JOAN MURRAY is a National Poetry Series winner whose books include *Dancing on the Edge* (Beacon, 2002), *Queen of the Mist* (Beacon, 1999), and *Looking for the Parade* (Norton, 1999). She is editor of *Poems to Live By in Uncertain Times* (Beacon, 2001) and general editor of the forthcoming *Pushcart Book of Poetry.*

PABLO NERUDA (1904–1973), the Chilean poet, won the Nobel Prize for Literature in 1971. His books include *Residence on Earth, Canto General,* and *The Captain's Verses.* A generous selection of his work is included in *The Poetry of Pablo Neruda* (FSG), edited by Ilan Stavans, which has just been published in paperback.

D. NURKSE is the author of eight books of poetry, including *The Fall* (Knopf, 2002) and *Burnt Island* (Knopf, 2005).

SHARON OLDS's books are *Satan Says; The Dead and the Living; The Gold Cell; The Father; The Wellspring; Blood, Tin, Straw; The Unswept Room;* and *Strike Sparks: Selected Poems, 1980–2002.* She teaches at NYU and helps run the NYU workshop at a state hospital for the severely physically challenged. She was New York State Poet Laureate from 1998–2000.

ISHLE YI PARK is a Korean American woman who is the Poet Laureate of Queens, New York. Her poems have been published in numerous anthologies, including *The Best American Poetry 2003.* Her first book, *The Temperature of This Water,* was published by Kaya Press.

MARGE PIERCY is the author of sixteen collections of poetry, most recently *Colors Passing Through Us* (Knopf), and sixteen novels, most recently *The Third Child* (Morrow/HarperCollins). A new CD of her political poetry, *Louder, We Can't Hear You (Yet)!,* is just out from Leapfrog Press, which also published *So You Want to Write,* co-authored with Ira Wood.

DANNYE ROMINE POWELL is a local news columnist for *The Charlotte Observer.* Her second collection of poems, *The Ecstasy of Regret,* came out in 2002 from the University of Arkansas Press. She has won an NEA and a North Carolina Artists fellowship, and she spent part of the 2004 winter at Yaddo.

LEROY QUINTANA, winner of two American Book Awards, was born and raised in New Mexico and served in the LRRPs (Long Range Recon Patrol) in the Vietnam War. He is author of *La Promesa and Other Stories* (Oklahoma) and the poetry collections *The Great Whirl of Exile* (Curbstone), *The History of Home,* and *My Hair Turning Gray Among Strangers* (Bilingual Press).

ADRIENNE RICH's most recent books of poetry are *The School Among the Ruins: Poems 2000–2004,* and *Fox: Poems 1998–2000* (Norton). A selection of her prose, *Arts of the Possible: Essays and Conversations,* was published in 2001. A new edition of *What Is Found There: Notebooks on Poetry and Politics,* appeared in 2003.

LUKE SALISBURY is a professor of English at Bunker Hill Community College in Boston. He is the author of the novel *The Answer Is Baseball; The Cleveland Indian,* nominated for the Casey Award in 1992; and *Blue Eden,* a collection of stories. A novel, *Hollywood & Sunset,* will be published this year.

VALERIE SAYERS, professor of English at the University of Notre Dame, is the author of five novels, including *Brain Fever.* Her stories, essays, and reviews appear widely.

ERIC PAUL SHAFFER's books include *Living at the Monastery, Working in the Kitchen* and *Portable Planet.* He publishes in *ACM, American Scholar, The North American Review,* and *The Threepenny Review.* He received the 2002 Elliot Cades Award for Literature. *Lāhaina Noon,* his fifth book of poetry, will be published in April 2005.

R. T. SMITH's collections of poetry include *Messenger* (LSU, 2001), which received the Library of Virginia Poetry Prize; *Brightwood* (LSU, 2003); and *The Hollow Log Lounge* (Illinois, 2003), which received the 2004 Maurice English Poetry Prize. He lives in Rockbridge County, Virginia.

GARY SOTO's most recent book is the young-adult short story collection called *Help Wanted* (Harcourt, 2005). He lives in Berkeley, California.

ILAN STAVANS is the Lewis-Sebring Professor in Latin American and Latino Culture at Amherst College. His latest books are *Dictionary Days* (Graywolf) and *The Schocken Book of Modern Sephardic Literature* (Random House). The paperback of *The Poetry of Pablo Neruda* (FSG), for which he was awarded Chile's Presidential Medal, is just out.

GERALD STERN is the author of fourteen books of poetry, including *This Time: New and Selected Poems*, which won a National Book Award in 1998. *Not God After All* was published in 2004 by Autumn House, and *Everything Is Burning* will be released by Norton in the spring of 2005. His essay collection, *What I Can't Bear Losing: Notes from a Life*, was released in 2003.

LIDIA TORRES's poems have been published in *The Massachusetts Review, Hayden's Ferry Review, Bilingual Review/Revista Bilingüe, Calabash*, and *The Beacon Best of 2000*. She lives in New York City.

LEWIS TURCO's most recent books, all published in 2004, are *The Collected Lyrics of Lewis Turco / Wesli Court 1953–2004, A Sheaf of Leaves: Literary Memoirs* (Star Cloud), and *The Book of Dialogue* (New England), companion volume to *The Book of Forms* and *The Book of Literary Terms*.

CHASE TWICHELL's new book, *Dog Language*, will be published by Copper Canyon in the fall of 2005. She is the editor of Ausable Press.

DAVID WILLIAMS has published two books of poetry, *Traveling Mercies* (Alice James, 1993) and *Far Sides of the Only World* (Carolina Wren, 2004). His work can also be found in many journals, including *The Atlantic Monthly, The Beloit Poetry Journal,* and *The Kenyon Review*, as well as in several anthologies.

IRA WOOD is the author of three novels, *The Kitchen Man, Going Public*, and *Storm Tide* (with Marge Piercy), all published by Ballantine, and the co-author of *So You Want to Write: How to Master the Craft of Writing Fiction and Memoir*. He is Associate Publisher of Leapfrog Press.

~

GUEST EDITOR POLICY *Ploughshares* is published three times a year: mixed issues of poetry and fiction in the Spring and Winter and a fiction issue in the Fall, with each guest-edited by a different writer of prominence, usually one whose early work was published in the journal. Guest editors are invited to solicit up to half of their issues, with the other half selected from unsolicited manuscripts screened for them by staff editors. This guest editor policy is designed to introduce readers to different literary circles and tastes, and to offer a fuller representation of the range and diversity of contemporary letters than would be possible with a single editorship. Yet, at the same time, we expect every issue to reflect our overall standards of literary excellence. We liken *Ploughshares* to a theater company: each issue might have a different guest editor and different writers—just as a play will have a different director, playwright, and cast—but subscribers can count on a governing aesthetic, a consistency in literary values and quality, that is uniquely our own.

SUBMISSION POLICIES We welcome unsolicited manuscripts from August 1 to March 31 (postmark dates). All submissions sent from April to July are returned unread. In the past, guest editors often announced specific themes for issues, but we have revised our editorial policies and no longer restrict submissions to thematic topics. Submit your work at any time during our reading period; if a manuscript is not timely for one issue, it will be considered for another. We do not recommend trying to target specific guest editors. Our backlog is unpredictable, and staff editors ultimately have the responsibility of determining for which editor a work is most appropriate. Mail one prose piece or one to three poems. No e-mail submissions. Poems should be individually typed either single- or double-spaced on one side of the page. Prose should be typed double-spaced on one side and be no longer than thirty pages. Although we look primarily for short stories, we occasionally publish personal essays/memoirs. Novel excerpts are acceptable if self-contained. Unsolicited book reviews and criticism are not considered. Please do not send multiple submissions of the same genre, and do not send another manuscript until you hear about the first. *No more than a total of two submissions per reading period.* Additional submissions will be returned unread. Mail your manuscript in a page-size manila envelope, your full name and address written on the outside. In general, address submissions to the "Fiction Editor," "Poetry Editor," or "Nonfiction Editor," not to the guest or staff editors by name, unless you have a legitimate association with them or have been previously published in the magazine. Unsolicited work sent directly to a guest editor's home or office will be ignored and discarded; guest editors are formally instructed not to read such work. *All manuscripts and correspondence regarding submissions should be accompanied by a business-size, self-addressed, stamped envelope (s.a.s.e.) for a response only. Manuscript copies will be recycled, not returned.* No replies will be given by e-mail or postcard. Expect three to five months for a decision. We now receive well over a thousand manuscripts a month. Do not query us until five months have passed, and if you do, please write to us, including an s.a.s.e. and indicating the postmark date of submission, instead of calling or e-mailing. Simultaneous submissions are amenable as long as they are indicated as such and we are notified immediately upon acceptance elsewhere. We cannot accommodate revisions, changes of return address, or forgotten s.a.s.e.'s after the fact. We do not reprint previously published work. Translations are welcome if permission has been granted. We cannot be responsible for delay, loss, or damage. Payment is upon publication: $25/printed page, $50 minimum and $250 maximum per author, with two copies of the issue and a one-year subscription.

THE NAME *Ploughshares* 1. The sharp edge of a plough that cuts a furrow in the earth. 2a. A variation of the name of the pub, the Plough and Stars, in Cambridge, Massachusetts, where the journal *Ploughshares* was founded in 1971. 2b. The pub's name was inspired by the Sean O'Casey play about the Easter Rising of the Irish "citizen army." The army's flag contained a plough, representing the things of the earth, hence practicality; and stars, the ideals by which the plough is steered. 3. A shared, collaborative, community effort. 4. A literary journal that has been energized by a desire for harmony, peace, and reform. Once, that spirit motivated civil rights marches, war protests, and student activism. Today, it still inspirits a desire for beating swords into ploughshares, but through the power and the beauty of the written word.

NATIONAL
ENDOWMENT
FOR THE ARTS

massculturalcouncil.org

IN MEMORIAM

JAMES RANDALL

1925–2005

Pym-Randall Press
Ploughshares
Emerson College
Ahab Rare Books

9th Annual

ZOETROPE: ALL-STORY
SHORT STORY WRITERS' WORKSHOP

SEPTEMBER 16 - SEPTEMBER 23, 2005

Come to Francis Ford Coppola's beautiful Blancaneaux Lodge in Belize for a weeklong writing retreat. Each day features small group workshops with instructors, guided writing exercises, and private writing time. Also included are four-star meals, luxurious bungalow accommodations, and trips to the Mayan ruins at Caracol, the Rainforest Medicine Trails, and the Rio On Pools.

BENNINGTON WRITING SEMINARS

MFA in Writing and Literature
Two-Year Low-Residency Program

A. BLAKE GARDNER

FICTION
NONFICTION
POETRY

CORE FACULTY

FICTION
Martha Cooley	Alice Mattison
Elizabeth Cox	Jill McCorkle
Amy Hempel	Askold Melnyczuk
Sheila Kohler	Virgil Suarez
Lynne Sharon Schwartz	

NONFICTION
Sven Birkerts	Phillip Lopate
Tom Bissell	Bob Shacochis
Susan Cheever	

POETRY
April Bernard	Ed Ochester
Henri Cole	Liam Rector
Amy Gerstler	Jason Shinder
E. Ethelbert Miller	

WRITERS-IN-RESIDENCE
Douglas Bauer	Lyndall Gordon
Robert Bly	Rick Moody
Donald Hall	

PAST FACULTY IN RESIDENCE
Agha Shahid Ali	Jane Kenyon
Amy Bloom	David Lehman
Lucie Brock-Broido	Carole Maso
Frederick Busch	Christopher Merrill
Robert Creeley	Sue Miller
Susan Dodd	Alicia Ostriker
Mark Doty	George Packer
Lynn Emanuel	Marjorie Perloff
Karen Finley	Jayne Anne Phillips
William Finnegan	Robert Pinsky
George Garrett	Robert Polito
Jane Hirshfield	Katha Pollitt
Barry Hannah	Alastair Reid
Edward Hoagland	Mary Robison
Richard Howard	Ilan Stavans
Marie Howe	Mac Wellman
Honorée Jeffers	

The Gettysburg Review côte d'Azur

SUMMER WRITING WORKSHOPS

19-25 JUNE, 2005

AT TOURRETTES-SUR-LOUP

A medieval village in the heart of the French Riviera
Workshops, Individual Conferences, Publishing Symposia in
Creative Nonfiction, Fiction, Poetry, Screenwriting

FACULTY

Jane Alison, *Fiction*

Khris Baxter, *Screenwriting*

Jonathan Dee, *Fiction*

Fred Leebron, *Fiction*

Robert Polito, *Poetry*

Kathryn Rhett, *Creative Nonfiction*

Liz Rosenberg, *Poetry*

Helen Schulman, *Fiction*

Tom Sleigh, *Poetry*

Peter Stitt, *Creative Nonfiction*

For information, contact
Kim Dana Kupperman 717-337-6774 or
kkupperm@gettysburg.edu or visit our web site at:
www.gettysburgreview.com

Dorothy Sargent Rosenberg
Annual Poetry Prizes

*Prizes from $1,000 to $25,000 for poems
by writers under the age of 40.
Deadline: November 6, 2005*

We now happily announce the 2005 Dorothy Sargent Rosenberg Poetry Contest, for which entries are due on November 6, 2005. The contest is open to all writers under the age of 40 on that date.

Prizes ranging from $1,000 up to as much as $25,000 will be awarded for the finest lyric poems celebrating the human spirit. All poets, published or unpublished, are eligible to enter, but only previously unpublished poems are eligible for prizes. Submissions must be in English: no translations.

Each entrant may submit one to three separate poems. Only one of the poems may be more than thirty lines in length. Each poem must be printed on a separate sheet. Please submit two copies of each entry, with your name and address clearly marked on each page of one copy only. Please also include an index card with your name and address, phone number, email address, and the titles of your submitted poems.

Entries should be mailed to Dorothy Sargent Rosenberg Poetry Prizes, PO Box 2306, Orinda, California 94563, to be received no later than November 6, 2005. Poems submitted will not be returned. Please see our website for further information: **www.DorothyPrizes.org**.

Notice of prize winners will be published on our website on February 5, 2006, and winners will be contacted shortly before that time.

There is a $10 entry fee and checks should be made out to the Dorothy Sargent Rosenberg Memorial Fund.

Prize winners for the 2004 competition, announced February 5, 2005:
$10,000 prize to Melisa Cahnmann
$7,500 prizes to Christopher Goodrich and Emily Rosko
$5,000 prizes to Nan Cohen and Tess Taylor
$2,500 prizes to Nicholas Mohlmann, Emily Orzech,
Tara Prescott, and Allison Seay
$1,000 prizes to Kathryn Hogan, Joe Kraus,
Amy Letter, and Dawn Lonsinger
There were also nine Honorable Mentions, at $100 each.
Thank you to everyone who entered and congratulations to our winners.

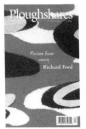